WALKING TOURS OF TEANECK

Larry Robertson

Full Court Press
Englewood Cliffs, New Jersey

First Edition

Copyright © 2016 by Larry Robertson and Judith Grace

All rights reserved. No part of this book may be reproduced
or transmitted in any form or by any means electronic or
mechanical, including by photocopying, by recording,
or by any information storage and retrieval system,
without the express permission of the author,
except where permitted by law.

Published in the United States of America
by Full Court Press, 601 Palisade Avenue,
Englewood Cliffs, NJ 07632
fullcourtpressnj.com

ISBN 978-1-938812-75-0
Library Of Congress Catalog No. 2016943780

Book design by Barry Sheinkopf for Bookshapers.Com
(www.bookshapers.com)

Colophon by Liz Sedlack

Dedication

To Judith A. Grace, my wife. All I had was a collection of facts and stories that would probably go with me when I die. Judy saw the need to turn my walking-tour notes into a guide-book for those interested in Teaneck's history who wanted to go on their own walking tours. She helped me overcome my considerable inertia and did a masterful job of editing, organizing, and motivating to get my stories into usable book form. Her knowledge of the English language, and her love of books, were the perfect ingredients.

Acknowledgments

I would like to thank Weilee Liu of the Teaneck Public Library for her help. Much thanks goes as well to Lucille Bertram, retired librarian, and Robert Griffin, historian, for their generous assistance over the years.

We are also grateful to Donning Company Publishers for their permission to reproduce the photo of the auto accident from p. 103 of *Bergen County: a Pictorial History,* to Imari Nacht, co-president of the Englewood Historical Society, for allowing us to use the illustration and map of the Lenape village from *This was Early Englewood,* by Dr. John K. Lattimer, and to the Berdan family to allowing us to reproduce images from their postcard collection

THIS BOOK IS BASED ON FOUR WALKING TOURS of Teaneck, so that, within each chapter, the information that follows is not a timeline but a physical route. The reader is invited to take a section, follow the accompanying map, and read the relevant text. Some information is repeated, as the reader may choose to do some but not all of the walks

Please note that, as a municipal historian, I make no comment on any issue more recent than thirty years; moreover, any opinions and/or statements in this book are strictly my own and do not reflect official findings of the municipality. Much of the information in this book is derived from primary sources, personal communications, maps, and official records.

In my opinion, changes in technology lead to developments in transportation, which lead to different land uses.

The Walks

River Road, pp. 3–24
Cedar Lane, pp. 27–52
Central Teaneck, pp. 55–91
Southeast Teaneck, pp. 95–133
Appendix 1: History of the Teaneck Fire Department, pp. 121–133
Appendix 2: Personal Railroad Memories, pp. 138-138

1

River Road

River Road

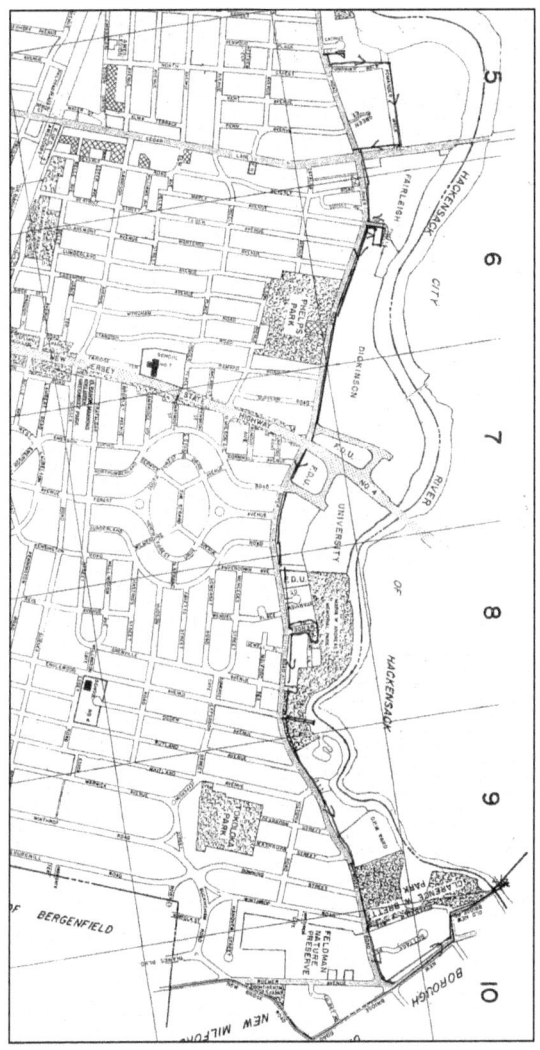

River Road Walk Map

Teaneck's original inhabitants were the Lenni Lenapes—later called Delawares by the Europeans.

The local branch were the Hackensackii of the Unami clan, who inhabited a large area of Bergen County. Two permanent settlements were located along Lindbergh Boulevard, one of which had about a hundred dwellings and a religious/municipal building called a "long house." They built on high ground to avoid the problem of sewage-borne diseases and for observation purposes. Basically a peaceful people with strong family and religious ties, they grew crops and medicinal herbs, and fished on Teaneck and Overpeck Creeks using "fykes," or traps—funnel-shaped netting composed of saplings. The Europeans adopted this practice but made the nets out of rope and eventually metal. When the creek ran vigorously after a rainstorm, fish, unable to swim out against the flow, would be caught in the fyke.

The Lenape built a fort on a bluff that overlooks a sharp bend in the Hackensack River. This installation, in today's Brett Park, marked the boundary between the Hackensackii and Tappans, two groups that had long-standing tensions and engaged in occasional warfare. New Bridge Road was built along French creek as a military road. Young warriors from the main village would be detailed to walk down the several miles to staff the riverine fort. Their job was to interdict any Tappan canoes attempting to cross the tribal boundary and violate their fishing rights. Excavations over the years have turned up many arrow- and spearheads from their in-ground armory.

The first Europeans to arrive in the area were more interested in trading with the local people than in oppressing them. The Winkelmann family had a trading post at the corner of River and Fort Lee Roads in Bogota. Beavers were very plentiful, and the Lenapes had developed the skills of trapping them and curing their hides. Beaver pelts would be bartered for knives (the Lenapes did not have iron-working ability), guns, alcohol, and clothing.

At first, the relationship between the Europeans and native people was harmonious; however, the policy of the Dutch company that ran the New Netherlands (the New York–New Jersey colonies) changed from an interest in trade to one of settling people in the area—not by seizing land, but by negotiation and purchase. But a major difference in the concept of land ownership existed between the two groups. To the Lenapes, property rights were for personal use, hunting, and fishing, but could not be transferred to heirs or resold. The European concept involved land ownership by the family to be passed on, sold, or even lost due to failure to pay taxes. There was no easy way to translate these differing concepts before Sarah Kierstadt, who developed a Dutch–Lenape dictionary. Governor Stuyvesant rewarded Ms. Kierstadt with a land grant that now includes all of Ridgefield Park and Bogota, and all of Teaneck south of Cedar Lane. While she continued to live in Brooklyn, her grandson occupied the land. His house still stands at 493 Teaneck Road.

Unfortunately, some dishonest settlers discovered that giving alcohol to the Lenapes before negotiating with them made things go better for the Europeans. Eventually, the Dutch governor, Van Kieft— a crooked politician who wanted to rob everyone—touched off a war. He was arrested, and Peter Stuyvesant became governor. He had the mind of a businessman and sought out Lenape leaders. He found Oratam, or Oritani—a "sachem" (or "sagamore") or judge—whom he also appointed deputy sheriff. Due to his dual offices, Oratam had the right to arrest both Lenapes and Dutch. He enforced alcohol prohibition laws for real estate negotiations, and he kept the peace. He lived into his nineties.

The last local tribal settlement, ending in the 1930s, was in Hackensack at 505 Main Street, behind Holy Trinity Roman Catholic Church. Some Lenapes intermarried with Europeans; most moved voluntarily in 1760 to the first Indian reservation—Brotherton, in Burlington County. The Lenapes had requested land so that they could continue their tribal life. This probably would have worked, except that the Quakers, who came from Philadelphia, wanted the same land.

Kipp-Cadmus House

The Kipp-Cadmus house at River Road and Cadmus Court is a good example of so-called colonial Dutch design. It was the house for an extensive farm that extended east from River Road and Kipp's Bend in the Hackensack River. Its architecture is typical of its time and contains a beautiful Dutch oven. Like almost all of its contemporaneous buildings, there are two dates of construction—one from before the Revolutionary War, and another from after. Bergen County was considered a middle ground, not controlled by either side, and was the site of continuous nightly raids that resulted in the destruction of all Teaneck houses with the exception of two blocks east of the Hackensack River at New Bridge Road.

The two movie houses that had existed in Hackensack for many decades—the Fox and the Oritani—were named for Lenapes. Fox, the last local Lenape chief, lived in the 1930s.

Another example of pre-Revolutionary riverfront farm houses is 1286 River Road, which had been the home of the Ackerman family in the 18th century. The small wing to the south was the original house, and when the farm prospered, the larger part was added. Like many houses of that era, two construction dates exist: the first, the original building date; and a second (generally about 1787), because almost all Teaneck buildings were destroyed during the Revolutionary War.

In the 19th century, the parking lot at Beverly and River Road was a cattle-watering pond. The land—not naturally dry—was suffused with small creeks, and local farmers led their dairy cows there for watering.

Cedar Lane did not continue across River Road into Hackensack as it does now. It made a T-intersection with River approximately where Beverly intersects River now. Currently, Cedar Lane makes a slight bend, so that it enters Hackensack aligned with Anderson Street. Until 1869, this did not matter, but subsequent to that the railroad built a station on Anderson Street in Hackensack, which spurred the construction of the bridge. Also, street names on the map would have been different. River Road north of Cedar Lane was East Hackensack Avenue, and, south of Cedar, it was Bogota Road. Cedar Lane itself was called Cedar Lane Road. Bogota was urbanized much earlier than Teaneck. Mail for South Teaneck was delivered there from the Bogota Post Office.

Until 1895, Cedar Lane was the boundary between Englewood Township and Ridgefield Township. Bergen County consisted of nine municipalities (now seventy) in the same area. The basic reason for the change was inferior municipal services. In 1894, if there was a fire on the corner of River and Cedar, the first fire engine would be coming from the east end of Main Street in Fort Lee—a distance of about five miles—yet they were paying the same tax rate as the people living a hundred feet from the same Fort Lee fire house. Other reasons, such as drainage and schools, gave rise to the number of municipalities we have now, enabling people to have a fair shot at getting the services they were paying for.

In the late 19th and 20th centuries, the area south of Cedar Lane and east of River Road used to be a horse-racing track covering the last two blocks of Penn and Kent Avenues down to River. It was a half-mile oval for sulky racing, which not only provided recreation for local residents but was an opportunity to see whether any horses for sale were healthy, smart, and manageable. Horse racing was common in a lot of Bergen County towns. When the motor age bumped out the horse era, the race tracks declined.

At the time that the first European settlers came to Bergen County, some roads had been established by the Lenapes, but these were neither all-weather nor reliable. The only avenues of transportation that could be relied on were rivers and creeks. The Kipp-Cadmus house, dating from before the Revolutionary War, was built right next to the river.

Once farmers got beyond the subsistence level and began to produce surplus crops for market, they would ship cash crops via the river and receive manufactured goods and building materials the same way. Working these farms was labor-intensive, and European families had many children to keep farms viable, but there was still insufficient manpower, and this led to the spread of slavery in Teaneck. Slavery, as practiced here, was not like that seen in the South. The number of slaves generally equaled the number of family members. They slept in the family house, in the basement or attic. In many of the houses that date from this era, metal rings can be seen embedded in the basement walls, to which slaves could be handcuffed as punishment. Slavery started to be abolished in New Jersey on July 4, 1804, due to state legislation, to be completely phased out by 1844. The forty-year delay was instituted primarily so that older slaves could live out their lives and not be discarded.

By the turn of the 19th century, the farmlands south of Cedar—by Larch and Elm—were the Harry Godwin orchards and were laid out for house lots by the Hackensack Land Development Company.

Pomander Walk was one of the first side streets in Teaneck. These streets started to be built in the late 1860s and represent a change in land use. In this era, commuter railroads were established in the area, and it became possible to live in Teaneck without being a farmer. The early commuters tended to be rich Wall Street attorneys and commodity brokers. They built large houses that were not farm houses. An important feature of Pomander is the cemetery at 662. This originally started as a Lenape burying ground. But when the Kipp family established a farm in the area, it also became a burial place for family members and farm workers, including slaves. It was legally designated a cemetery and was shown as such on maps up until 1936. In the 1950s, a shady developer bought part of the Kipp estate for housing. Somehow

Cemetery at 662 Pomander Walk

he made the cemetery designation disappear, and houses were built on top of the burial ground. Fortunately, part of it was not developed, and thanks to tenacious local residents, this area has now been re-designated as a cemetery and is owned by Teaneck.

Fairleigh Dickinson University (FDU) took over Bergen Junior College after World War II. The mansion of State Senator Abraham Collard existed where FDU's Linden dorms #1,2,3 currently stand on a rise above the Hackensack River. This was the first house in Teaneck to have electric light, but only around the outside of the building, not the inside. Lighting was installed to deter hit men hired by local shipping interests, because Collard had proposed damming the Hackensack River in Bogota to form a recreational lake. This would have prevented schooners and barges from continuing upriver to service industries as far north as Oradell.

Banta-Coe House, 884 Lone Pine Lane

One of the few remaining 19th-century mansions of the type that used to line the bluff between River Road and the Hackensack River is at 884 Lone Pine Lane. They were built in that location in order to make maximum use of cooling breezes in the summer and to avoid the downhill flow of sewage, since township sewers were not established until 1920. Most the houses became classroom or dormitory buildings for Bergen County Junior College in 1942 and then passed into the hands of FDU and were eventually torn down.

We think of traffic as a current day problem, but in the 1930s, the intersection of River Road and Cedar Lane was the most frequent location for traffic accidents in Bergen County (*see next page*).

At the corner of Martense and River on March 14, 1926, a Teaneck policeman died in the line of duty when the side-car motorcycle in which he was riding collided with a horse-drawn milk wagon in the

Auto accident, Cedar Lane and River Road, c. 1920

early morning. Three line-of-duty deaths have occurred in the Teaneck Police Department.

North on FDU's property (near Ramapo Road), two important local industries were established in the 19th and early 20th centuries. One was the property of John Jay Phelps, who had a large house called Red Towers. He also owned greenhouses, which had started out as a hobby but developed into a wholesale florist business with local and New York City customers. Across the street lay the property of Sophie Henderson, who owned Henderson Seeds, a mail-order seed company also based on greenhouse operations.

John Jay Phelps (*see next page*), the son of William Walter Phelps, who was the major landowner and developer of Teaneck in the 19th century (more about him in the Cedar Lane section), had a mansion with a wharf along River Road, near Ramapo Road, for tying up his

Lieutenant Commander John Jay Phelps, 1898

private schooner, which he used for worldwide yachting operations. He was a naval veteran of the Spanish-American war.

Street names have meanings. If we proceed off River Road to Wendell Place to Academy Lane, we would have encountered Roosevelt Military Academy (*see next page*), a private high school in the early 20th century that provided military training as well as academics. Academies of all types flourished until the late 1920s because of the scarcity of public high schools. By the 1930s, public high schools were common enough that most academies went out of business.

Looking west from Academy Lane, we notice Teaneck Pond, also known as Indian Pond . This was man-made and is kept filled by river water at high tide by means of a clapper gate. Up through the 1960s, it was a popular nighttime ice-skating location—illuminated by railroad

Roosevelt Military Academy

flares and supplied with large kettles of soup and hot chocolate. Currently, it is used by part of Teaneck's Jewish population to cast their bread upon the waters as part of an annual religious observance.

On River Road, opposite Rutland Road, lies the Lutheran cemetery, founded at the site in 1702 as a part of the Church in the Woods, established by the Van Buskirk family, which, like many "Dutch" settlers, were not really Dutch. They were Germans from East Friesland who changed their name to Van Buskirk to reflect that they were affiliated with the "church in the woods" (as translated literally from the Dutch). This church was unusual in Bergen County in that it was the only Christian congregation of its time that was not part of the Dutch Reformed sect. Its members also tended to back the British when the question of American independence arose. As a result, the church became vacant at the close of the Revolutionary War. Local people who had backed the British had to leave or face an unpleasant fate. Having stood empty for many years, the church was destroyed in 1820 by a local grass fire. There was no fire department at the time. The cemetery remained and is still so designated, until the 1930s, many 18th-century headstones were still visible. The devastating hurricane of September 1938 produced a storm surge that gouged out the land and floated remains and stones downriver to be lost forever.

Lutheran cemetery

Department of Public Works (DPW) Yard. Before this area acquired its present use, it belonged to the Cole family, which operated a lumber and coal facility. At first, the lumber was grown locally and dragged by horse teams to the yard, where steam-powered saws and planes turned it from timber into dimensional lumber. This was shipped downriver by schooner and was used in the building of Newark, Jersey City, and other rapidly urbanizing areas. The returning schooners carried coal, which had arrived—from the Scranton, Pennsylvania, area via the Morris Canal—at this yard, where some was used to power the machinery and some sold to locals for domestic heating and cooking. Later, lumber was imported through the yard and sold locally to feed the local building boom.

If we look along River Road in front of the DPW, we see a monument commemorating a sewerage plant that existed there until the 1950s. Between 1920 and 1950, Teaneck operated five sewer-treatment plants to remove biological and other contaminants so that the water could be released into the river. The initiation of the Teaneck Municipal Sewerage System, which occurred in 1920, was a life-saving improvement. Before that, local residents had dumped sewage onto the ground, which on occasion found its way into neighbors' potable water wells. As in many communities, the deaths of infants and children from cholera, typhoid, and even yellow fever were common in Teaneck. Until 1920 and even afterwards, some neighboring municipalities continued to dump untreated sewage into the Hackensack River, from which water was pumped to provide Hackensack swimming holes. This contributed to the polio outbreak in the early 1950s.

River Road and Riverview Avenue. Before there was a municipal school district, there was a unified county school system. One county grammar school stood on the northwest corner of Riverview Avenue and River Road. When the school districts were created to conform to municipal boundaries, this school became surplus and stood vacant. During the Prohibition Era, producers of banned alcohol sought industrial sites in Bergen County, because county prosecutors of both parties forbade local police from enforcing the liquor laws. One enterprising group obtained use of the school. They cut out large sections of the first and second floors and built a towering copper-still complex. This was in use until alcohol became legal and was then abandoned. A fire set by juvenile delinquents in 1940 brought the fire department to the building. Upon entering, they were amazed to find that it was really a concealed industrial complex with a weakened structure. When another fire was set, the firemen stayed outside, wary of a collapse. To avoid blocking River Road for a prolonged period, they built a suspension bridge of fire ladders and rope to carry fire hose across the road—an innovation that gained nationwide notice in fire trade publications.

New Bridge Road

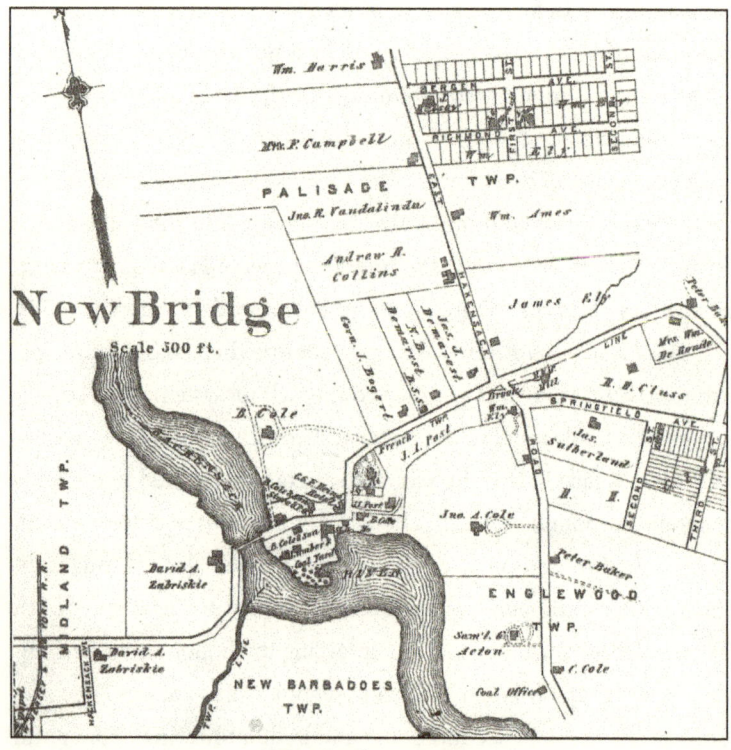

New Bridge, c. 1876

New Bridge Road is packed with history. The thoroughfare had existed for possibly hundreds of years before it acquired its current name. Originally, it was a Lenape patrol road. Between 1742 and 1746, a stagecoach route from Hackensack to the future Hudson County was planned and built. As part of this effort, a new bridge was constructed across the Hackensack River, together with an inn to accommodate passengers.

Until 1791, New Bridge was the southernmost bridge over the Hackensack River. "Old Bridge," which existed prior to this, was at River Edge Road in New Milford.

On November 20, 1776, British soldiers and their German allies secretly crossed the Hudson River opposite Alpine with the intention of surprising and capturing or wiping out the six thousand American soldiers garrisoned at coast artillery positions in Fort Lee.

In 1776, Germany was made up of three hundred separate states, kingdoms, counties, and city-states. Several of them rented whole regiments of infantry and cavalry to the British Empire. Most came from Hesse–Kassel, so people took to calling them "Hessians."

The original New Bridge Inn, built in the 1740s

Thanks to the bravery of local residents, the American garrison received warning in the nick of time and had to immediately evacuate the fort. Many soldiers only had time to take their muskets. Few had eaten. Many were barefoot—even naked. The two regular escape routes could accommodate only a few hundred soldiers each. The bulk of the garrison had to escape northwest along New Bridge Road to reach the southernmost available bridge across the Hackensack River, so that they could continue the evacuation.

New Bridge, 1880s

A German light infantry captain, Johann Ewald, scouting in front of the British forces, spotted the American column moving west along New Bridge Road near Prospect Avenue. He sent a non-commissioned officer back to contact Brigadier (later Major General) Cornwallis, better known for having surrendered to American forces at

Yorktown, Virginia, who was in charge of the Fort Lee invasion force. Hauptman Ewald urged him to bring his forces forward and end the war in one stroke. Cornwallis disagreed, and the Americans had just enough time to get across the bridge. They knew they had to further delay the British pursuit but lacked the explosives to blow up the bridge. Since they had only hand tools, they could only pull up the bridge deck, not destroy the larger stringer beams beneath. So they posted an eight-man squad in houses on the Teaneck side, armed only with muskets and a limited amount of ammunition. The rest of the militia platoon dug into the tall grass next to what is now the von Steuben House. In the gloom of that rainy late afternoon, the leading British and German elements reached the disabled bridge. The 42nd Highlanders were ordered to slowly pick their way across the beams to secure the opposite bank. Other units piled into the area where the snipers were concealed. The snipers fired all of their ammunition while the rest of the platoon poured several volleys into the congested forces. When the ammunition ran out, the eight Bergen County militiamen on the Teaneck side did not stand a chance. They were surrounded, outnumbered, and had no bayonets. All were captured, and none survived the deadly British prison ships in New York harbor. But the time that they bought allowed Washington's troops to cross Bergen County on the way to safety in Pennsylvania.

Another interesting note about New Bridge Road: On July 13, 1895, when the Cherry Hill tornado touched down at the south end of River Edge and crossing into Teaneck, it collapsed buildings, thereby trapping, injuring, or killing residents. There were no local public emergency services in existence. The only bit of good luck was that a railroad track maintenance crew happened to be present and managed to extricate some of the victims. This absence of organized rescue services inspired the New

Bridge Road neighbors to found Defender Hook and Ladder, based in Teaneck at 722 New Bridge Road in an amazing one-month period. The company went into service on August 13, 1895.

Teaneck's only "maritime" disaster occurred in the winter of 1888 in the Hackensack River at New Bridge. A schooner was moored to the wharf of the Zabriskie brothers' grain business. It was used to deliver finished flour to the market in Newark and was needed immediately for a large shipment, but cold weather had locked the hull of the ship with ice. The Zabriskie brothers had recently fired their longterm schooner captain and hired a local fishermen, who had a lot of river experience but none with schooners. When he found the ship iced in, he went to the New Bridge Inn and asked the local river men what to do. They suggested pouring kerosene on the ice around the hull, but they did not say anything about igniting it. The rookie captain lit the kerosene, and the schooner, the *Katie B. Lawrence*, burned to the water line. Ribs of the ship were still visible at low tide until the end of the 20th century.

Cedar Lane

CEDAR LANE

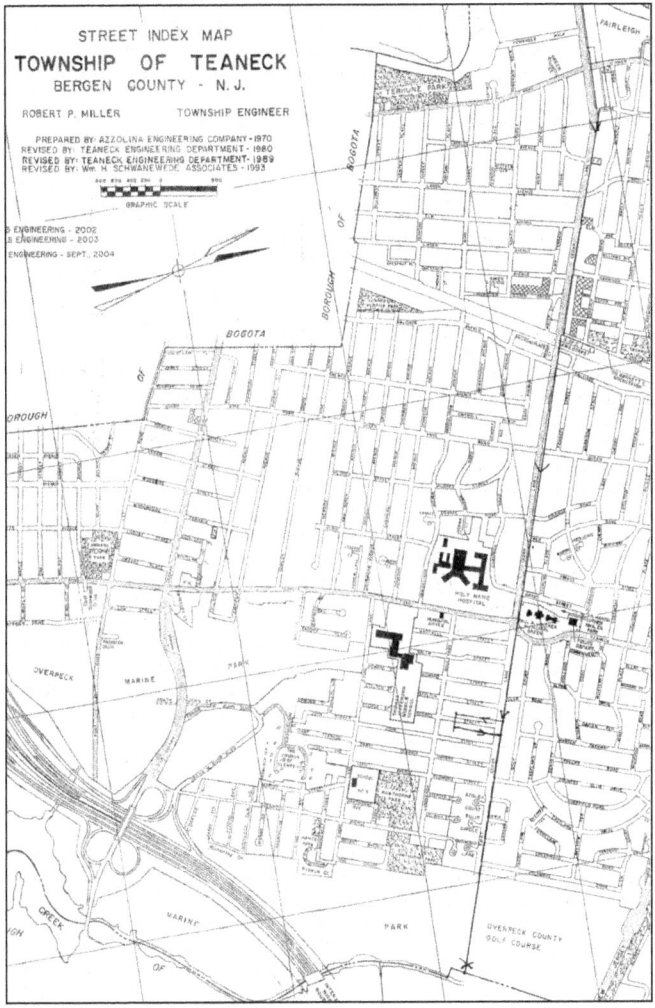

Cedar Lane Walk Map

To BEGIN WITH, PLEASE NOTE THAT, in taking this walk, *you will need to be in a car* when you reach the golf course gate east of Columbus Drive, because the golf course staff bans pedestrians from entering.

Cedar Lane used to run straight and end at River Road and Beverly. There is now a curve in the road between the two Catalpas. Only in 1861 did any consideration begin for a bridge to Hackensack. When county authorities finally elected to build one in 1869, they wanted to bend Cedar Lane so that it aligned roughly with Anderson Street in Hackensack. The current bridge was constructed in the 1970s and replaced a steel-truss bridge from 1888 that could be opened to allow river shipping to pass.

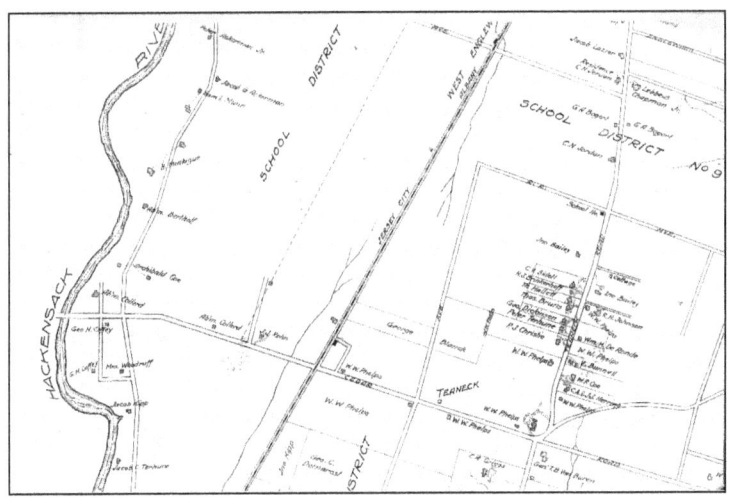

Cedar Lane in 1876

Cedar Lane was laid out as a street in the European sense in 1744. There's a part—East Cedar Lane—that predates it by an unknown number of years and was used by the Lenapes to access their main village. Cedar Lane was not the main business district until 1927; however, some retail stores existed there. The first one, owned by Abraham

Billings' store and fishing boat

Collard, was in a house at 837 Cedar Lane rented by Charles Billings.

He and his wife, who were both born in New Jersey and had ten children, appear on the 1895 tax record. Their business was to sell the fish that Mr. Billings caught in the river and vegetables raised on the plot. The 1900 census showed that all of their children over the age of sixteen had jobs. One was a coachman, another a domestic workers, etc. All were successful and paid a poll tax, which indicated that they voted. They also had a dog license. They were black. So among the first Cedar Lane merchants were a black family. They later got a franchise to sell Breyer's Ice Cream. Other major businesses were a dairy at 205 Cedar Lane and a blacksmith at 207—the current Teaneck Shell station. These business pioneers were Scots and Germans.

Before 1895, south of the center line of Cedar Lane was Ridgefield Township, and north of it was Englewood Township.

In the 19th century, behind the rows of current Fairleigh Dickinson University dorms, stood an expensive house owned by Abraham Collard, a state senator. His idea was to place a dam across the Hackensack River opposite Court Street in Hackensack, with the purpose of stopping it from being a tidal waterway. He intended to set gypsum in the river to settle the salt and sewerage to the bottom, so as to make a recreational lake and turn the houses into resort hotels, thus increasing the value of the properties along River Road.

This idea was popular with large landowners but was poison to the people who depended on the river to deliver their coal and grain. So Collard became the target of a murder plot. Killers were hired to get him. In self-defense, Collard installed the first electric lights in Teaneck, mentioned earlier. The outside of his house in the 1880s was illuminated by calcium arc lamps, i.e., limelight. A coal-fired boiler in the basement made steam, which drove a generator, which lit the lamps. Every night the outside of the house was brightly lit to discourage intruders.

Pomander Walk was one of Teaneck's first side streets. In the 1870s, there were only five side streets—others are now called Aspen, Spruce, Balsam, and Fycke Lane. Pomander Walk was built as access to several mansions erected around 1869. Walter Bound owned most of the land and sold lots to other wealthy families. A family named Coffee was one of the main purchasers. Luisa Moore had a French chateau-style home, which was torn down to make Classic Residence. Its significance was that it was the beginning of suburban development from farm lands.

River Road is an old street, one of the original Lenape lanes. It had several names in the 19th century—north of Cedar Lane it was East Hackensack Avenue and also the Public Road; the southern part was called Bogota Road. Bogota was urbanized earlier than Teaneck. The names lasted almost until World War I. Parts of the road were washed out by a hurricane, rebuilt by the county, and re-named River Road.

Opposite 647 Cedar Lane lies the curve that was introduced to accommodate the 1869 bridge. Nine houses on the north side of Cedar Lane between Catalpa and River at about 709 Cedar were made to look "old." One of these houses (which one is not known) actually is older and had been rented by a Reverend George C. Holland, who was assistant pastor in Mt. Olive Baptist Church in Hackensack. He was well known at the time for his sermons.

Casa Mana

Until 1964 there was a nightclub, famous in the New York metropolitan area, called the Casa Mana at 647 Cedar. A man named Emile Fore operated a large garage there, which serviced telephone company and mail trucks and was subsequently turned into a nightclub after the end of Prohibition. A race track for sulkies (across from Casa Mana, south of Cedar) existed at Penn and Kent Avenues in the late 19th and early 20th centuries.

Catalpa Avenue was the marshaling area for a victory parade by the (Nazi) German-American Bund in the summer of 1940 to celebrate Germany's victory over France and the Low Countries. The parade went up Cedar Lane to the corner of Palisade Avenue. A color movie of it exists. Some prominent Cedar Lane merchants at the time were German-American, and the Bund was strong here. Their leader, Fritz Kuhn, lived on the Boulevard and Main Street in New Milford. After the Madison Square Garden Bund meeting of 1940, World War I veterans ambushed Bund members getting off the ferry in Edgewater. Someone had called the local police, who found a large group of people slugging it out with baseball bats. Allegedly, the first Edgewater cop who got to the scene reported back, "Nothing going on here."

There was a fire station from 1913 to 1953 at 513 Kenwood Place, currently Chabad House. Before that, the fire company that protected southwest Teaneck rented a barn at 519 Linden Avenue.

If you took this walk in 1925, you would have been tired out by the hill (in the 500 block of Cedar) that used to continue and crested at Linden Avenue to about the third-story level. In 1927, a decision was made to level the hill, for two reasons: one, to provide soil for another public works project (raising the level of Cedar from Water Street to Palisade Avenue in order to pass over the railroad tracks on a bridge), and two, to make Cedar Lane a more viable shopping street. The project was accomplished by a large number of Norwegian immigrants who came to the United States because of a depression in Norway in the 1920s. They leveled the street by hand with picks and shovels and used mules to carry away the soil. This brought the street down about fifteen to twenty feet,

Teaneck Station seen from Cedar Lane

to shale. Try to imagine this area as a wooded hill.

In 1865, William Walter Phelps bought the Brinkerhoff farm (they had been the first Europeans to own the land). Which at the time was being offered by a realtor from Jersey City—Henry Fink—who sold him the core of the estate. Between 1865 and 1894, Phelps built it into an empire. Any time someone offered him land, he bought it at whatever price they asked, and then hired most of those people back as estate workers. He wound up owning one-third of Teaneck, Englewood, and Englewood Cliffs, with interests in Hudson County and Connecticut. Only the Brinkerhoff farm was used as such. The name of Grange Road reflects this—a grange being a threshing floor. Threshing was done at Grange and Merrison. The rest of the land was rented out to other farmers or was used as a private park.

One of the compensations for working for Phelps was housing. In the 19th century, Red Road had a row of houses all painted dark red or maroon—the color of all Phelps' buildings. He was known for being

William W. Phelps

a good boss who treated his workers well.

Phelps was the son of the man who had founded the Delaware, Lackawanna and Western Railroad. His father had started out as a working class person who became a cloth merchant, then a lawyer, and had gotten into railroads as they were first becoming important. Phelps did not participate in the Civil War because of a problem with his lungs, which eventually caused his early demise and was the impetus for his buying land in New Jersey to escape the polluted conditions of New York City.

The current municipal complex was the heart of the Phelps estate. His mansion was a long, irregularly shaped building, constructed out of the original farm house that resembled a Swiss chalet. It had fourteen fireplaces, measured eighty by three hundred feet, and varied in height from one to two and a half stories. Phelps worked as a Wall Street attorney and filled his home with art purchased in his travels.

William W. Phelps mansion, before 1888

Phelps mansion in ruins, 1888

He served in the government and became the first United States minister (as ambassadors were then called) to Austria-Hungary, then Prussia. His daughter, Marion married the Foreign Minister of Germany, Count Rotenberg.

There were no gas company pipes to provide lighting, so the house had a calcium-carbide acetylene generator in the basement in which water dripping onto the calcium carbide produced acetylene, which was piped throughout the house in fixtures that were similar to gas lights. At night, the water was turned off so that the acetylene would not be produced. One burner was left on at night to consume the excess and had to be turned off before starting the generator the next day. Prior to the night of April 1, 1888, someone forgot to turn off a light fixture. As it grew toward evening, more calcium carbide was loaded. The two-storey library and art gallery filled with acetylene before anyone noticed it. Phelps was in Washington, DC, fulfilling his duties as a US Congressman; his wife and daughter were at home.

Finally, someone smelled gas. William Bennett, the estate manager (similar to today's township engineer), was summoned from next door. When he opened the door, the acetylene rushed out and hit another source of fire, perhaps a lamp, exploded, and caught fire. The building burned slowly. Estate workers pitched in and saved a lot of contents, which were put into the stables—where the Jewish Community Center is now located—which also began to burn from the radiant heat. There was no fire department in Teaneck because there was no official township yet. The Englewood Fire Department was responsible but their apparatus was hand-drawn. A ride alerted them, but they had to draw their engine up huge hills to get there. Another rider went to Hackensack and pulled a fire alarm box where Sears is now.

The horse-drawn Hackensack fire apparatus arrived first but also struggled with the steep, muddy hills. They were able to save the stables. One Hackensack fire fighter was injured when he overreached and fell from a ladder, knocking burning shingles off the side of the barn while a hose line was being established. A very long stretch of hose tapped into the mill pond where Thomas Jefferson Middle School is now. The injured fire fighter was given first aid by Phelps' daughter.

Phelps had been alerted about the fire by telegram and came home on the afternoon train. A three-storey mansion belonging to C.R. Griggs, a New York cotton broker, stood across the street from the mansion (currently. The core of Holy Name Hospital). Phelps asked the price, peeled off the cash, and immediately bought that house, where he and his family lived out the rest of their lives.

In 1922, when Mrs. Phelps moved back to Connecticut, the land went to the hospital courtesy of Grace Chadwick. The manager. William Bennett, who had discovered the fire, survived and became Teaneck's first mayor. Phelps' sons, J.J. Phelps, later a captain (actually, lieutenant commander), fought in the Spanish American war. Before that, he had developed an interest in growing flowers as a hobby. Eventually, he turned this avocation into a commercial enterprise with greenhouses originally at 885 Teaneck Road, with more at 1000 River Road, and a retail shop.

The Phelps estate played a small but important role in preparing New Jersey's citizen soldiers for the world war to come.

In 1902, U.S. Congressman Dick of Ohio forced legislation that improved the National Guard in response to troop performance in the Spanish-American War. The quality of military units in that war varied from terrific to quite poor for both citizen and regular army. So an effort was made in the 1903 Act to improve training and material preparations. It changed the name of the militia to "National Guard" and created equal ranks—which means that the same standards to become a non-commissioned or commissioned officer were imposed on all branches of the military. Thus, an army sergeant would be comparable to a sergeant of marines or the National Guard. It also required all branches of the armed forces to engage in maneuvers on a unit size greater than battalion (at that time about six hundred men). Some units were deficient in basics such as where to dig latrines so as not to pollute the water supply, and how to cook food. In the Spanish-American War, many more soldiers died from disease than battle.

International tensions had been rising, as evidenced by the Fashoda and Agadir incidents and ethnic turmoil in the Balkans. In Russia, the Romanovs were under attack from within. More importantly for New Jersey's troops, America had recently defeated the Spanish empire and acquired colonial possession in both the Caribbean and Pacific. In the Philippines, besides having to fight a local insurrection, there was a potentially serious confrontation with the Imperial Germany Navy.

While New Jersey units performed adequately in national maneuvers at Manassas, Virginia, in 1904, the officers of the 5th New Jersey Infantry were concerned enough to plan a regiment-sized battle drill.

In May 1906, the Adjutant of the 2nd battalion, 5th New Jersey Infantry, First Lieutenant John W. Loveland, approached William Walter Phelps' widow and was generously awarded permission to use the wide and varied expanses of her estate for a military exercise. Strict safety rules were issued, copied from regular army practices, and six captains who were West Point instructors were engaged as field umpires and evaluators.

The premise of the war game was that a foreign army had landed in Newark and was trying to attack Connecticut. An important logistic base, the Englewood Armory at Armory Street and Englewood Avenue, was to be defended by the Bergen County Battalion. If the attackers had placed at least forty soldiers within six hundred yards of the armory by 4:00 p.m., the attackers would be considered the winners.

The invading army, wearing brown uniforms, were the Essex and Passaic battalions of the 5th New Jersey Infantry—now the 113th Infantry—who rode by trolley to Hackensack. They dismounted from the street cars at Anderson and Main Streets and proceeded east on Cedar Lane. As you will remember, few side streets existed at this time. Their mission was to simulate an invasion from Newark and capture Nyack, New York.

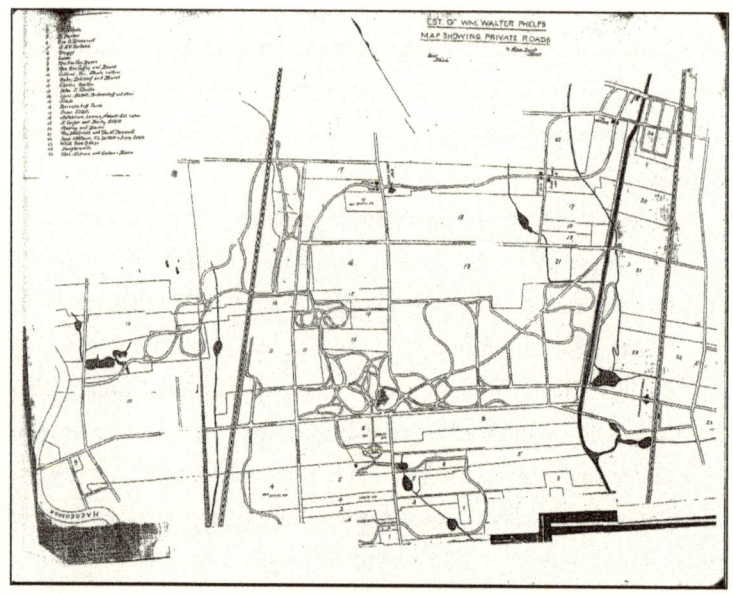

Phelps private roads

The defender, the Bergen County battalion, had asked for a cavalry screen, because then, as now, cavalry is put out in front of infantry to feel out the enemy, to determine the direction in which they are going, and to confuse them. The cavalry from Jersey City that was supposed to work with them was not available; so infantry from Bergen County rented touring cars, onto which machine gun mounts were welded, and created the first mechanized cavalry in the world. This was eight years ahead of the regular army, which adopted the innovation only in 1914.

The cavalry screen—a thin line acting as a detector of the enemy's presence and intentions—was established on the Linden Avenue hill. When the "enemy" got there, the first contact (with blanks) was between the Bergen County cavalry screen and the Essex County infantry. The cavalry, detecting the approach of the enemy, fired some blanks, causing a delay in the enemy advance while they scooted back to the main line of resistance near Teaneck Road to report the encounter.

The invaders stopped at a candy store and bought a commercial local street map, but the defenders relied on government military maps. On the local maps, the invaders found that local streets— Heasly Avenue (now Palisade Avenue) and Teaneck Station Road (now Cherry Lane) offered a way around the defenses. The official government map did not show this. The invaders correctly expected the main line of resistance across either East Cedar Lane or East Forest Avenue. They found Heasly Avenue, then Teaneck Station Road. A company of the Brown Army (invaders) was designated as Flank Guard, and they followed the local streets, then traveled along the ridge above Teaneck Road until they reached a Phelps riding trail named Glade Road (now Genessee Avenue). This road was not shown on the official 1903 government maps, and Company G of the defending battalion had done a poor job of covering the approaches along the west branch of the Overpeck Creek. Using the local maps, the invading force bypassed the main line of defense at East Forest and Cooper, and engulfed and captured the Englewood armory by about 11:00 a.m.

The West Point instructors harshly criticized the Bergen County troops for failing to maintain contact between various small units placed side-to-side in the defense, and for placing infantry troops right in front of their own artillery, rendering the guns unsafe to fire. These failings were, however, a blessing in disguise, because the privates and second lieutenants in this exercise were the senior non-commissioned officers and field-grade officers who led New Jersey men in the great test to come in 1917–18. Who knows how many lives were saved by the Phelps Estate maneuvers of 1906?

The property from the Provident Bank to the Hanna Nail Salon was referred to as the Leer's building. Leer was a businessman from Bogota who bought the two plots of land for $600.00 in 1933. Across the street is Garrison Avenue. Samuel Garrison was a contractor from the Rochester area of New York State. In the 1880s, he had been hired by the railroad to work in the vicinity of where the line is now. He constructed bridges and culverts.

He started his own business and so became Teaneck's first homegrown contractor. He owned a large house at Garrison and Beatrice, which burned in the 1930s.

The first kosher merchant was a poultry store at 405 Cedar.

The Lakeland Bank Building had previously been a Buick dealer, then an Acme market, and then an auction house. After the gangster Albert Anastasia was shot in a Manhattan barber ship in the 1950s, his possessions were auctioned there, in a sale so well attended that the fire department had to clear the building.

In 1873, the Ridgefield Park Railroad was constructed from the Midland railroad line (now the Susquehanna) in Ridgefield Park to Madison Avenue in Dumont. It was a very local operation —two locomotives, two passenger cars, two freight cars. It went out of business but reappeared in 1876 as the Jersey City and Albany Railroad. It was later bought by the West Shore Railroad and operated from Weehawken to Buffalo, New York. Eventually, it was purchased by the New

York Central, since Cornelius Vanderbilt considered it a threat to his Harlem and Hudson River lines. It is now the CSX River line. It has gone through good and bad times. One of the good times was 1926. They had so much business that they wanted to expand from a two- to a four-track line to be able to build up a good amount of speed for express trains. The owners met with municipal officials in Bogota and Teaneck to eliminate road crossings. It became a long process—from 1926 to 1938. Part of this process involved raising the grade of Cedar Lane.

Originally, Cedar crossed the railroad track at grade, then went up a very steep hill toward Queen Anne Road. The plan was to replace the grade crossing with a bridge. The soil from the Linden Avenue hill project was trucked two blocks east, and a dirt ramp was built upward from Front Street (now American Legion Drive) to an elevation equal to the grade of Palisade Avenue. Then a bridge was constructed to connect the ramp and Palisade Avenue.

As part of the ramp and bridge project in 1926, the Hackensack Water Company redirected its thirty-inch water main down Water Street, underneath the railroad tracks, and up Manor Court. This is how Water Street got its name and shape. Meanwhile, the New York Central Railroad rented the machinery that had been used to build the Panama Canal and employed it to lower the grade of the tracks in central Teaneck and raise the grade in the swampy area where Votee Park is now. They eliminated the road crossing of Cedar Lane over the railroad tracks.

In 1938, Teaneck closed the West Englewood Avenue crossing in lieu of the 1926 bridge at State Street. Forty-eight passenger trains a day went through. It took less time to get to New York City than it does now. From the Teaneck station-– originally at the foot of Cherry

Lane, later at Frances Street-- you could take a train to Albany then a through-train to Chicago. They converted from steam to diesel in the 1950s. This writer's first household chore was to remove the soot from the window sills in his family home.

Heasly Avenue (the old name for Palisade Avenue) ended at Cherry Lane (in 1894 called Teaneck Station Road) and was built by Phelps for direct access to the station from his house. The original station was behind where Limone's farm recently stood.

Standing on Cedar Lane between Palisade Avenue and Queen Anne Road, a traveler can look south and see a fifteen-foot-high raw dirt embankment, the top of which contains the rear yards of houses on Barr Avenue and represents the original grade of Cedar until 1889. After the delayed response of the Hackensack Fire Department to his mansion fire of 1888, Phelps contributed money to lower the hill to where it is now and pave it with crushed stone. He then donated the steam roller used in the paving as a shared asset of Englewood and Ridgefield townships.

On top of the hill, southwest of Cedar Lane and Queen Anne Road in the late 19th and early 20th centuries, stood the Fiss, Duerr, and Carroll horse farm. This was a horse and vehicle rental facility that grew to include a program to recruit, train, and sell horses to pull urban street cars. During World War I, this company shipped out artillery horses to the French and Imperial Russian armies. With the end of World War I and the coming of automobile, the facility was vacated, and it was destroyed in an arson fire in 1919.

Until 1922, Queen Anne Road was known as Westfield Avenue. Just east of Queen Anne were two of the three original Cedar Lane businesses. At 209 Cedar in the 1900s, William Robertson had a blacksmith shop, and Henry Boehne's retail dairy, which was probably part of the original Phelps estate, stood at 205. At first they milked the cows there, but by the 1960s, pasteurized milk was trucked in and broken down for sale. The store burned in 1962, the same night that the *U.S.S. Constellation* did in the Brooklyn Navy Yard.

In 1900, the entire ten-thousand-foot length of Cedar Lane — from River Road to the golf course—was illuminated only by seven gasoline-fueled street lamps. Hot items in the minutes of the town council at the turn of the 20th century included complaints about the poor work of the street-lighting contractor. Other neighborhoods had electric street lights, but Cedar Lane didn't because it was not a commercially important street. Fort Lee Road and Teaneck Road were more significant.

Cedar was a not principally a business street until the planners in 1927 decreed it. From 1744 to 1927, the real purpose of Cedar Lane was to tie together settlers on both sides of the Teaneck ridge.

There had been a steep hill from Palisade to Queen Anne Road, which was paved with cobblestones to give horses hoof-hold traction. The hill was steeper before the 1880s. Grace Chadwick, who had owned a mansion in the 1900s (now the CVS store at 188 Cedar) in the 1920s, donated the land and money for Holy Name Hospital and St. Marks' Church (118 Chadwick Road).

On the site of the current Volks Funeral Home (789 Teaneck Road) stood the residence of General Van Buren, a light infantry militia officer in the Civil War. His daughter, Edith, was very liberated for her day, took an unescorted tour of Europe, and, unfortunately, became the victim of a marriage scam to get her money. In Italy, she went through a sham wedding with a fake priest to a man who told her that he was the Count di Castelmenardo. When she returned to Teaneck, she kept the title of Countess even though it was fictitious. The house later became a famous road house called the Blue Bird Inn. Another restaurant, called the Palm Gardens, existed at 819 Teaneck Road. Both were legitimate businesses that offered dancing; they were also big-time speakeasies, which were infiltrated by the mob from Hudson County. A large dance hall, part of the operation, stood on the lawn of the current hospital and was arsoned in a spectacular fire in 1932. The arsonist took chicken bladders from the restaurant, filled them with gasoline, tied off the ends, and stretched them over the necks of light bulbs as the incendiary device. He was caught by the Teaneck Fire Department.

Between August 22 and 23, 1780, about two brigades (about 1,200 soldiers) of American infantry encamped on what is now the Holy Name Hospital parking lot. The Americans had been pushed around by the British for about four years. After receiving good discipline, drills, and training from Baron von Steuben, and receiving equipment from the French through Lafayette, the rebels had started to become an effective army, and by 1780 were beginning to force the British out of Bergen County, which was a terrible place to live during the Revolution. British forces were very strong. They killed a lot of local people and burned buildings and crops. So it was heartening that the American forces were having an effect after four horrible years.

East Cedar Lane predates the rest of the street. In 1922, when Teaneck established a street address system, the "east" designation was intended to distinguish addresses across Teaneck Road. The section from Teaneck Road to River Road became a street under the British Colonial authorities in 1744; however, this area had been inhabited for hundreds of years before the Europeans came.

The Lenapes had a large village centered at Lindberg and George, off Cedar Lane, and extending down John Street, probably to Fyke Lane, with two suburbs. The Lenapes depended on river products,

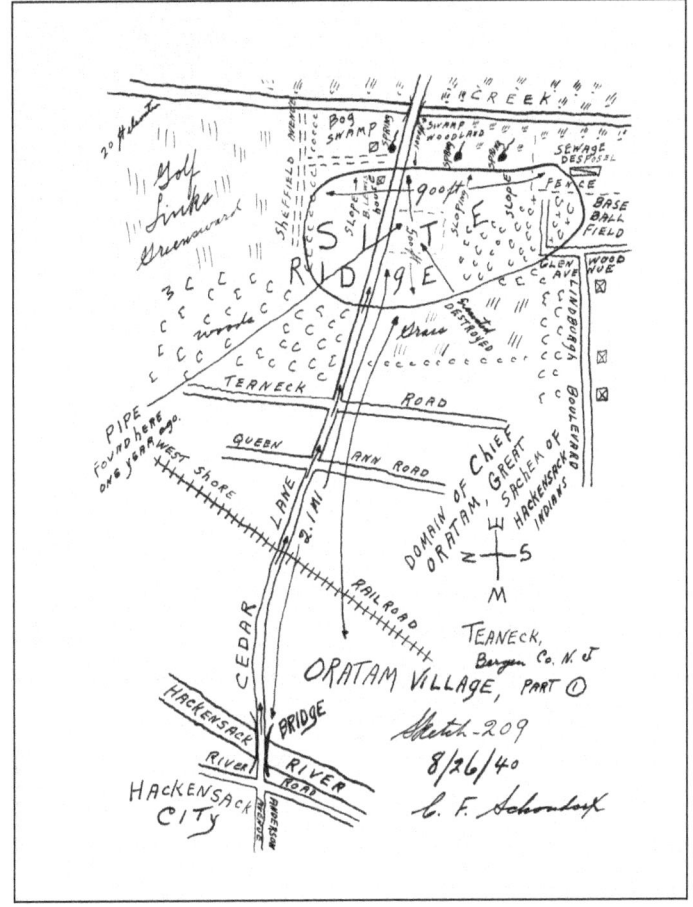

Oratam's Village map, drawn by C.F. Schoonmaker in 1940

such as shell fish, and they used East Cedar Lane to get to the Overpeck Creek, or Teaneck Road to New Bridge Road to the Hackensack River.

The village consisted of about six hundred "wikkiups," semi-permanent structures made of bent saplings covered with bark. They did not have tepees like the Plains Indians. They built on a hill for sanitary

Lenape wikkiups

purposes.

Lenapes used creeks for fishing. They installed a fish trap that was funnel-shaped and woven out of twigs. When the water ran fast on the Teaneck or Overpeck Creeks, the fish would swim into it and not be able to escape, because very few fish carry pocket knives. They also collected shellfish from the Overpeck Creek, which remained a tidal estuary until 1894, when Bergen County built a tide gate under the Bergen Turnpike on the Ridgefield Park/Ridgefield border. The Lenapes also grew squash and grains, harvested nuts and berries, and probably did some hunting. They main source of protein, however, was fish.

East Cedar Lane was their main access to Teaneck Path—the connection between them and the Tappan Indians when they were not at war. It also provided access their other village at River Road. It is likely that the name "Teaneck" comes from the Lenape word "Utenek", meaning "place of the villages". Another possibility is that the source is a common Dutch name "Tenyek". There's a Tenck Street in the Greenpoint section of Brooklyn.

Chief Oratam

The most prominent member of the Lenapes was Oratam—a Latinized version of his name. If he lived today, his address would be in the 700 block of George Street, as it was the center of the Lenape village. In addition to the smaller wikkiups, they had a long house that served as a government building and a place of religious assembly. Oratam probably lived adjacent to that. His rank was "sachem," which translates to "judge". Like the ancient Israelites, who had judges as their leaders, the Lenapes invested in the main executive authority the power to settle disputes. Hackensack uses Oratam's seal in its own, but there is no evidence that he lived there. He lived in Teaneck.

The Lenapes had the first reservation in the United States, but it was not like the others, because they joined it voluntarily. It was at a place called Brotherton, on the Delaware River in Burlington County, New Jersey. Around the 1760s, they had a choice of integrating with the Europeans or keeping tribal ways. Some Lenapes are still around locally.

The Brotherton reservation operated well enough until the Quakers arrived. They wanted the land and stole Brotherton from them by manipulating the New Jersey legislature. The Lenapes were then relocated to Ohio, which is not very different topographically from New Jersey. More settlers came and pushed them out again, and the Lenapes ended up in Oklahoma, which is completely different. They lived a terrible life in Oklahoma until they discovered oil. Many who stayed here became iron workers, like the Mohawks, and worked on New York skyscrapers.

In 1643, war broke out between the Lenapes and the Europeans, mainly due to governmental stupidity. The Dutch governor for New York/New Jersey was Willem Keift. He had some strange personal habits and was a thief. The Mohawk and Hackensack Indians went to war, which raged in this area. The Hackensacks thought that the Dutch were friendly to them, because they had good trade relations. They rushed down to Jersey City and sought entry to a Dutch fort for protection from the Tappans. Governor Keift let them in but then ordered the guards to fire into the crowd and killed them all. When word reached the Lenapes, they wiped out the Dutch settlements at Winkelmans—now Bogota—a ninety-foot fur trading post on the corner of Fort Lee and River Roads, and also Vriesendahl, a waterfront fishing village in Edgewater, around the foot of Dempsey Avenue.

East Cedar Lane was a through street to Englewood from 1744 to the 1950s, when an association of private sanitation contractors in Teaneck took control of the land as a garbage dump and closed the street. At East Cedar Lane and Hartwell Street, a sign read *Cedar Lane ends in _____ feet;* the number changed frequently in the 1950s. The author would frequently come down to see how long Cedar Lane was that day.

Until the 1930s, East Cedar Lane was the site of a famous golf course attracting world-class tournaments. The street names here—Country Club Road, Golf Court, Club Road—reflect this. The course was killed by the Depression.

This was also the site of the John H. Lewis farm—one of the last of three working farms in Teaneck. The others were Limone's (at 892 Palisade) and Reikow Brothers, opposite Downing Street on River Road. In 1948, it became more profitable to sell the land, so many farms went under. Mr. Lewis was very elderly by that time and could not keep up the house.

Street names. The "magic" number to get a street named after you was ten acres. Lewis was one of the few who had a street (Lewis Court) using his last name.

In 1894, Englewood paid to have the Overpeck Creek straightened out and to embank it, thus turning it into a drainage canal to prevent flooding downtown. The aim was also to use it for coal and lumber barges. The cost of constructing this sanitary canal angered the Teaneck taxpayers, who were then part of Englewood Township. The residents of River Road, Heasly Avenue, and so forth resented a big tax increase for a project that benefited only downtown Englewood. This caused those residents to join with the people from Ridgefield township, at the south end of our existing town, to form the current Teaneck.

Before that, the Overpeck Creek was irregularly shaped and had a mill—Van Horn's mill in the 1790s. Even at that time it was said to be an ancient tide mill, so it was probably one of the first of the European mills that used water power to grind grain into flour. Van Horn did not have a bridge but a low-head dam. On November 20, 1776, the Revolutionary army, which had almost been surrounded and cut off in Fort Lee, beat a hasty retreat from the British, who had crossed the Hudson River at Alpine and come down the northern valley. Most American troops retreated via downtown Englewood, New Bridge Road, and the New Bridge. Others went through Little Ferry and used the ferry, but two hundred soldiers were caught in a traffic jam. In English Neighborhood—now Grand Avenue, Englewood—some broke away and crossed the dam at East Cedar Lane. A regiment of state marines from Massachusetts patrolled and took soldiers who had not made it across the Hackensack River on ferries. It is possible that these Marblehead Marines rescued soldiers at the foot of Cedar Lane. They then scuttled all boats to deny their use by the British.

Van Horn's mill was replaced by a flour bleachery in the 19th century. Next to it stood Barrett's dye works—not exactly a very healthy placement. There was a bridge at the foot of Sheffield Avenue, which remained in use until the 1930s. Both were destroyed by brush fires in the 1960s, by which time they had stopped being road bridges.

3

Central Teaneck

CENTRAL TENECK

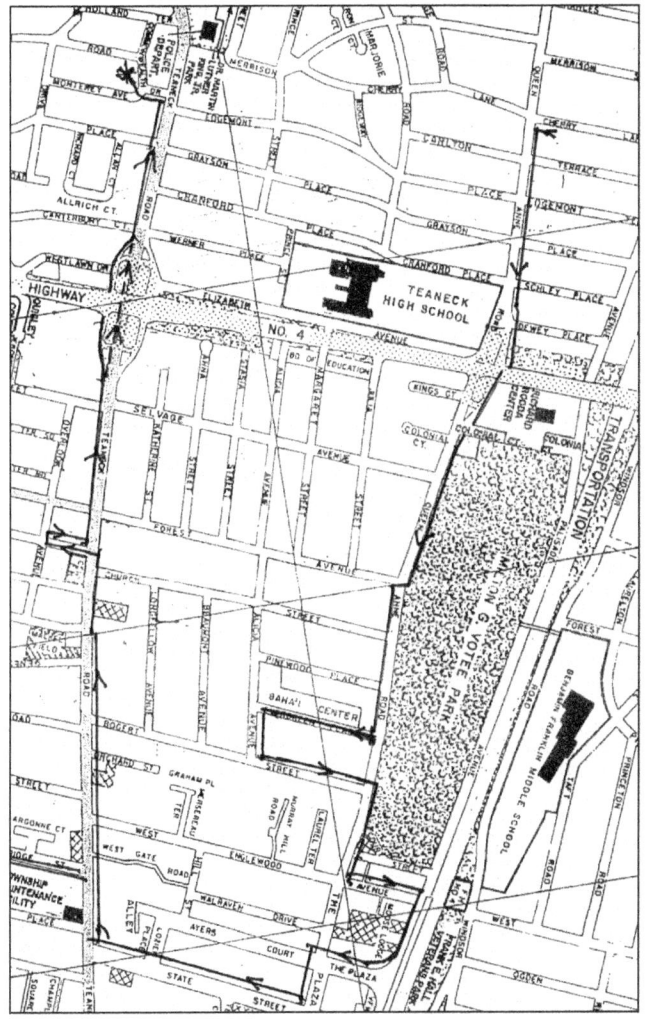

Central Teaneck Walk Map

If we were standing at Queen Anne Road and Cherry Lane in 1900, we would have been looking at a dirt road. It was called Westfield Avenue until the 1920s. The cross street, Cherry Lane, was Teaneck Station Road when Teaneck became a municipality in 1895; before that, it was a private road on the Phelps estate. Phelps had hundreds of miles of roads, some dirt and some gravel. Cherry Lane existed for the passenger railroad station at the back of the estate, near where Limone's farm (892 Palisade Avenue) used to be. Phelps had a hobby of planting trees. He used different kinds of trees to line various roads—so Cherry Lane had Oxford cherry trees, which are now long gone, but some of which lasted into the 1940s. He added about six hundred thousand to his estate in Teaneck, Englewood, and Englewood Cliffs. Even though he was in poor health (he suffered from lifelong emphysema), he rode out on the tail board of the tree-planting wagon and helped as much as he could.

The two-car garage at 890 Queen Anne Road had an unusual history. It was destroyed by two plane crashes within the space of ten years. The first was on May 25, 1942 *(see next page)*. The United States was at war. The Army Air Corps was flying combat air patrols above the metropolitan area, looking for the enemy. Two planes—both P39s, each fully loaded with .50-caliber machine guns—had taken off from Newark Airport. Flying in a two-plane formation above Teaneck Road and State Street, they encountered very high winds, which caused the planes' wings to touch and go out of control. One flew over Teaneck High School, where the collision activated the firing mechanism for the wing machine guns. Armor-piercing, incendiary bullets

890 Queen Anne Road, airplane crash, 1942

hit forty-two houses from near Teaneck Road and Bogert to Cherry Lane and Queen Anne Road. No one was hit, but a Bogert Street resident had a coffee cup shot out of his hand in his kitchen.

One plane came straight down and landed in the yard of 1090 Dartmouth Street, by Northumberland Road. The gas tanks burst open, and gasoline splashed onto a bed in a second-floor bedroom where a little girl was sleeping. Fortunately, it was a cool day in May, she had several blankets, and the fire stayed on top of them, so she managed to slither out safely.

The other plane crashed into the 890 Queen Anne Road garage, set it on fire, and also destroyed two almost-new cars with new tires, which were a real treasure in 1942 because civilian production had ceased and car tires were not available. The warplane crushed the garage and touched off a gasoline-and-rubber-fueled inferno.

The pilots did not fare much better. Both managed to bail out, but the high winds were still a problem. One parachuted down onto the high school athletic field, which did not have a fence around it as it does now. Landing in a parachute is a tricky business. To prevent the wind from re-inflating the chute after landing, two straps called "risers" should have been pulled to the ground. The pilot did not do this, and a gust of wind dragged him across Route 4 at high speed. There were no Jersey barriers then, just four-inch curbs. He hit his head hard against the curb at Route 4 and Julia Street. A woman, known to this historian, who was a nursing student and worked as a nurse's aide at Columbia Presbyterian hospital in New York, was coming home from her night tour, saw the pilot hit his head, and realized that he was going to lose his airway. She hurried to the front of the bus and demanded to be let off. The driver pointed to the signs about not talking to the driver and being let off only at designated stops. She told him that he was going to be on the street next to the pilot if he didn't let her off. The driver jammed on the brakes, and she saved the pilot's life.

Although uninjured, the second pilot faced death in different circumstances. He alighted on the lawn of the Teaneck Armory, which was a full-time, federalized military installation with barbed wire around it, and was guarded by new soldiers with very little training or experience. Just imagine the scene. There were no two-way radios. The soldiers heard a loud bang, continuous machine-gun fire, and two more bangs. They saw columns of smoke, heard the air raid sirens and the fire department recall horns go off, as well as all kinds of apparatus speeding somewhere. Out of the sky, a man in a black leather uniform then came down in a parachute. Their first thought was that he might be a *Fallschirmsjager*, a German paratrooper. Two sentries ran over.

They did not have ammo but did have fixed bayonets. They tried to stab the guy as he rolled around on the ground yelling things that only an American would know—World Series results, state senators, etc. A master sergeant soon rushed out and stopped everything. This part of the story was suppressed at the time.

Teaneck had a very good civil defense organization, which then sprang into action. The Teaneck Fire Department and ambulance corps had conducted a drill a week before the plane crashes, with the same scenario, about a block away from the actual incident. This historian has spoken to responders who were there and said that the drill enabled them to deal calmly with the event.

The other fire incident was controlled by citizens with hand-pump fire extinguishers and garden hoses until the fire department arrived.

The second plane crash occurred in 1952. A civilian plane, a single-engine Beaver business plane, took off from Newton, Massachusetts, with three people on board, bound for Teterboro. The pilot did not know that their altimeter was defective and showed them two to three hundred feet higher than they actually were.

There used to be a large Dutch elm tree on the northwest corner of Cherry and Queen Anne. One of the approaches to Teterboro is right overhead, so the pilot was on the right path, but he flew too low and crashed into the tree. The engine broke loose and set fire to a garage. The people in the plane were removed by the fire department but were beyond help.

We were ready in 1962 for the next event, but nothing happened.

Three streets were built, and a fourth was planned, to commemorate the naval heroes of the Spanish-American War of 1898. Grayson Place was named for Private William Grayson, who was the first soldier to fire a shot in the Philippine Insurrection.

Schley Place was named after the naval commander of the American Atlantic squadron that was in charge of the whole Caribbean campaign for the navy in the 1898 war.

Dewey Place was named for Commodore Dewey, the commander of the Pacific squadron that took Manila Bay from the Spanish. There was another street that was never built because of Route 4, which was to be called Hobson Place, for a naval lieutenant who bravely sank a coal ship, or collier, in the throat of Santiago de Cuba harbor, forcing the Spanish Atlantic Squadron to sally one ship at a time.

Right now, there are four vehicular crossings of the railroad in Teaneck—at Cedar Lane, Grayson Place, Route 4, and State Street. The bridges on Cedar and Route 4 date to 1926 and 1929, respectively.

The Grayson Place Bridge dates to 1873. It has been rebuilt four times. In 1873, the railroad—then called the Ridgefield Park Railroad—coming through Teaneck was intended to connect Bergenfield, Dumont, Teaneck, and Bogota to the Susquehanna tracks in Ridgefield Park, which was then the New Jersey Midland Railroad, going east-west. In order to do this, they had to buy the land, because they did not have power of eminent domain, and proceeded to bargain for it. Most people were happy to sell, because they saw an increase in property values. One farmer, named George M. Blanck, did not see it that way (*see next page*). The area near Queen Anne Road was the upland pasture for his dairy cattle during the day. At night, they were in a barn where Sagamore Park is now. Blanck had no objection to the railroad but was afraid that his cows would get hit by a train. He would only sell his land if the railroad built him a bridge. It was an expensive undertaking, but the railroad did it because they needed the land. It was constructed, not at the foot of Grayson, but instead a block north, from Schley Place to Birch Street.

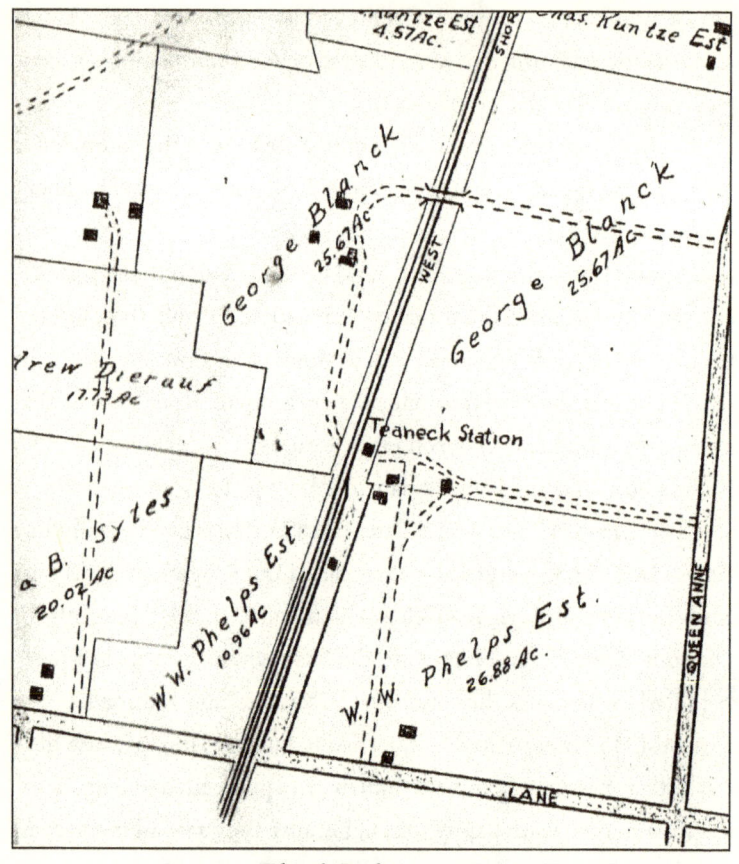

Blanck Bridge, c. 1873

The original bridge burned down. The first locomotives burned wood, not coal, which produced a lot more embers. A second bridge also was damaged by fire. Eventually an iron bridge on the Grayson Place–Sagamore Avenue alignment was built in about 1926, when the railroad expanded from two to four tracks. The present bridge was constructed in 1968.

The original streets—East Cedar Lane, Teaneck Road, New Bridge Road, and River Road—were based on Lenape trails. More streets (including Cedar Lane) were added in the 18th century, but until about 1926 the street map essentially consisted only of main streets. There were no side streets until after the railroads came.

Teaneck developed much later than the neighboring towns in relation to municipal services, sewers, and street addresses. Bogota developed twelve to fifteen years ahead of it, Hackensack about fifty, and Englewood about thirty.

In the 19th and early 20th centuries, a dairy farm belonging to Charles Kuntze existed where the Rodda Center is now. The farm morphed into a small industrial complex after the farmer decided that parts of the slaughtered cattle were going to waste. So he began a soap factory, which used the bones and fat, and installed a tannery for the hides. After the farm, the site became the Clausen Moving and Storage Building, which lasted until the 1970s.

A few words about Teaneck High School. In the 19th century, public schools in New Jersey were by run by the county. There are currently proposals for county-wide school districts—it's been tried before. Legislation in the 1880s and 1890s allowed municipalities to form school districts, which, as of 1894, were required to have the same borders as municipalities. This allowed the townships and boroughs to become what they are now. The original regionalization was a failure. People wanted more control.

Teaneck started to have municipal schools in 1895. There were not enough students for a high school, so, depending on where you lived in Teaneck, you went to high school in Hackensack, Leonia, or, eventually, Bogota or Englewood—all of which were populous enough to have public high schools. Many kids went to private high schools, which at the time were not generally religious, just not public. A military academy that was a high school existed on Academy Lane, Wendell

Place, and River Road in Teaneck.

By 1929, Teaneck had enough students in justify a high school. The school board bought the land that the high school currently occupies. It was a wooded lot. To keep expenses down, the board held a party in the winter for anyone with the skills or proper equipment for land clearing—farmers, construction workers, and homeowners with saws. Those unable to do the heavier work came equipped with vats of soup and hot chocolate to keep the job going. The land for the athletic field was cleared, even of stumps, in one afternoon.

The center and south sections of the high school were built with local tax money. When the Depression came, that was no longer possible. So the north wing of the high school was built by FDR's Works Progress Administration—a quasi-military labor corps whose leaders were reserve commissioned and non-commissioned officers. The WPA also did interior work on the other wings. As a result, Teaneck High School had more decoration than would most. A good example are the gargoyles that hold up the beams in the hallway. The stone owl over the clock in the center section was an add-on by the WPA, as were the cement bleachers. There was no graduating class until 1932.

Teaneck High School had something unique—in the 1930s and 1940s, an aviation program that trained pilots, mechanics, and aircraft designers. The first instructor was Major Arthur G. Norwood, a World War I veteran. The program started with a glider going down Werner Place.

They had Link trainers, which were cockpits set up in classrooms on trunnions (an axle-mounting on a stand balanced by gyroscopes that could simulate flight—*see next page*). A Teaneck High School airplane was quartered in Teterboro airport and one of the heroes of that program was Dorothy Fulton. In 1937, flying back from a training

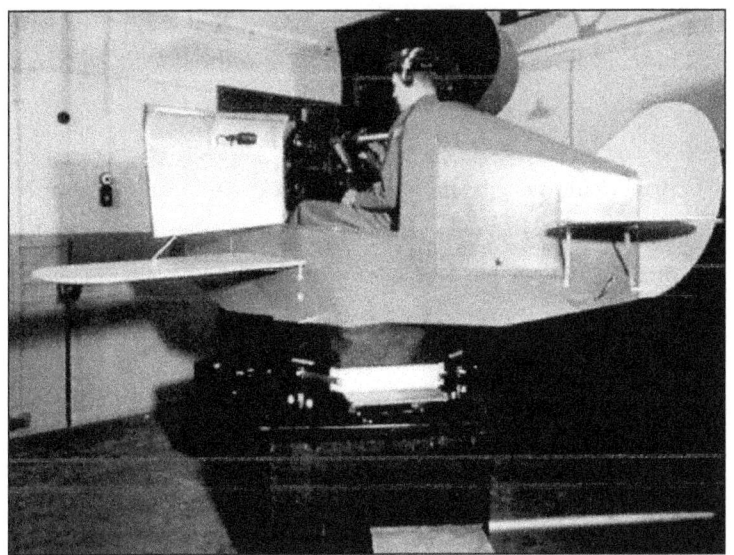

Link Trainer

flight, her plane lost its propeller over Cedar Lane and River Road. She made a dead-stick landing, i.e., with no power and just using ailerons and rudder, and landed at Teterboro. She became one of the ferry pilots in World War II who took nearly completed war planes either from Teterboro or Newark airports and flew them across the Atlantic with no armaments, right through the German naval patrol aircraft. In Britain, the planes were equipped with armaments and used in the war. Thirty to forty years later, such women were recognized as part of the military and granted the same rights and benefits.

Many Teaneck High School students who were in the aviation program joined the Royal Canadian Air Force, the Royal Australian Air Force, the Royal Navy, or the Royal Air Force before American entered World War II. Others jointed the U.S. Army Air Corps or U.S. Navy or Marine aviation after 1941. The program disappeared in the

1950s. At one time pictures of all these heroes were in the main hallway, but they were removed in the 1960s. One thousand people, out of a population of twenty-nine thousand in Teaneck, were on active duty.

Teaneck individuals who were in the program included Corporal Robert A. Rockefeller, who was killed in action in the South Pacific on a mission as aerial photographer, and Lieutenant Walter Echwald, who was with Air Transport Command.

Women's Air Force Service pilots include Patricia Thomas and Kay Monges, who ferried war planes to ports of embarkation.

By 1944, three hundred and fifty students were enrolled in the program, of whom one hundred and forty became military air crew. The rest worked in war plants. Teaneck High School had the highest number of representatives in military aviation of any high school in New Jersey. Bergen Junior College, which became Fairleigh Dickinson University, had twenty-five men in military flight training for glider pilots. The gliders were built in Ridgefield.

Changes in technology lead to changes in transportation and land use. The most remote was the knowledge of how to control fire to make a log into a canoe, as developed by our first inhabitants, the Lenapes. Then, in the 16th century, Europeans developed better ocean-going vessels and the navigation skills that brought the first wave of European immigrants and their African slaves. The 1850s brought railroads: In 1859, the railroad that goes through Englewood; in 1860, the north-south commuter line through Hackensack; in 1871, the Susquehanna, which goes east-west through Bogota to Paterson; and, in 1873, the CSX river line through Teaneck.

The railroads initiated Teaneck's evolution from a farming community to a "bedroom" community—but only for the wealthy. If you had an eighteen-room house, three servants, and a job on Wall Street or downtown Jersey City, you could afford to be driven to a railroad station in a one-horse platform-type carriage (i.e., a "station" wagon) and be picked up in the evening. Your house was not a farmhouse. You might have a few chickens or a goat or a vegetable garden, but you did not need a ten- or twenty-acre farm.

In 1876, the Teaneck street map started to show side streets. On the 1837 map, there are none. Side streets came off Cedar Lane and Englewood Avenue.

There are very few differences between the 1876 and 1920 Teaneck maps; basically, there were patches of farmland connected by a few main streets.

The 1926 map looks like the current map, without Routes 80 or 95. What happened? The George Washington Bridge.

From 1860 to 1934, a trip to New York began on a rail line from Hackensack, Englewood, or Teaneck to Hudson County, and a transfer to a ferry or, later, to the Hudson Tubes (subsequently the PATH trains). Another possibility was the DeGraw Avenue trolley, which brought passengers to a ferry across to 125th Street in Manhattan.

People had been agitating for a bridge across the Hudson since 1867, mostly demanding access from Hudson County to Midtown. An architect named Othmar Ammann, who lived in Teaneck for a time, came up with the idea for the George Washington Bridge, since it would easier and cheaper—it would not involve large approach ramps like the Brooklyn Bridge. It could connect Fort Washington and Fort Lee and would be very strong because it would be anchored to the Palisades on both sides. He eventually convinced the Port Authority to adopt his idea. The ten-to-twenty-acre farmers did not need much convincing to exchange their world of mud for rows of houses.

As it became known in the 1920s that the bridge was to become a reality, the municipality started to be transformed. In 1920, sanitary sewers replaced cesspools. In 1922, street addresses were developed. House numbers were of significance, especially in the urbanized portions of Teaneck where there were three people on the same block, all named Smith. In 1920, paid members were added to the fire department, and, in 1926, a purpose-built municipal building was constructed. Previously, a former school at Teaneck Road and Church Street had been used.

Walter Selvage was a big developer. His first project was the original Manhattan Heights development, east of Teaneck Road to Englewood, and from Route 4 to Bedford Avenue. As this was a success, he built in 1909 along Queen Anne Road to Teaneck; this was called the Selvage Addition.

He also owned the land where Votee Park is now but did not build on it because it was a swamp and providing drainage would have been very expensive. Before anything else could be done with the site, World War I began, and all manpower and materials went to the war effort. In the 1920s, before the stock market crash, the land was sold to others with the intention of building seven streets with one-family houses, but the cash for the construction project was not forthcoming; so, like many a swampy place in Teaneck, the area was seized by the municipality for back taxes. Milton G. Votee, who was the mayor in 1930, saw an opportunity. He was familiar with Central Park in New York, and as this acreage was pretty much central in Teaneck, he planned to turn it into a park. At the time, there was only one other in Teaneck, Townhall Park, which was right behind the municipal building.

To induce citizens to come to the park, Mayor Votee applied to the quasi-military construction force called the CCC (Civilian Conservation Corps). It had a camp in Teterboro, which it had just drained. The work on Teaneck was all done by hand, with picks, shovels, and wheelbarrows. The first drainage line they installed was pitched a quarter inch to the foot, going up instead of going down. So the initial work had to be redone, and it took months and months for guys up to their waists in mosquito-ridden mud. The amphitheater was one of the original constructions, and the basic drainage and some of the small culvert bridges that go over creeks were done by the CCC. It became Teaneck Central Park in 1934; in the 1970s, the name was changed to Votee Park. Argonne Park, between Forest and Englewood Avenue, had a similar history, as did Tokaloka Park.

A lot of original houses are still around in Teaneck; most of the housing stock is from about 1927. In 1948, a different design came in with another wave of building. Europeans had been here since 1630 and had very large farms, which gradually got smaller until 1865 or 1870. There was only one street in Teaneck that was not occupied by farm buildings—two sections of New Bridge Road, an original commercial neighborhood. In the 1870s, things changed because of rail transportation.

This is the Baha'i Center, a religious center similar to a church, synagogue, or mosque (*see next page*). Baha'i started in Iran in about 1836 as a reaction to Islam. Baha'i U'llah, the founder, synthesized several religions, mainly Christianity, Judaism, Zoroastrianism, and Islam. He was violently suppressed in Persia, and his son took over the movement. The son contacted a very wealthy man, Roy Wilhelm, a coffee importer who lived at 1234 Alicia Avenue in Teaneck. At some point in his travels all over the world to find coffee, he had encountered Baha'i and become a member. Wilhelm persuaded Baha'i's son to

Baha'i Center

come to the United States, which he did in 1912. In that building, the garage of the caretaker's house, the 1912 touring car used to travel around the United States and start Baha'i centers is still on view. The headquarters of Baha'i, in Chicago, is a reinforced concrete structure, one of the first in the country. Wilhelm deeded his land and the building at 126 Evergreen Place, built between 1912 and 1933. It's a true log cabin, not just built to look like one. Meetings and religious educational activities take place there, and, once a year, a regional gathering occurs to commemorate the visit of Baha'i U'llah's son. The building was designed by Louis Bourgeois, a New York stationery store owner who had a stand in the building where Wilhelm worked. At the time there was no specific training to become an architect. Bourgeois also designed his own house at Bogert Street and Alicia Avenue.

Streets in the Selvage Addition were all named for family and friends: Katherine, Anna, Stasia, Alicia, Margaret, and Julia.

Bogert Street is one of the older side streets. The Bogert family was one of the original European settlers. We think they were really French, but everyone says Dutch people came here up to 1664 under Dutch authority and needed Dutch papers. Some were Dutch; others came from countries in which it was illegal to be Protestant, e.g., France, Poland, and some states in Germany. So we see names like Zabriski (really Sobiewski) and Demarest (really Demarais).

The Bogerts proliferated in Bergen County. Bogota was named after them because at one time almost every resident was a Bogert. They were prominent in architecture, engineering, and construction. Bogert Street in Teaneck was probably named after Samuel Bogert, a builder from Englewood when this was part of Englewood Township. Houses that have concrete or poured-concrete foundations are newer—generally constructed before 1910 but far more recent than ones with brick or stone foundations, which are original. In 1910, Portland cement became available as a construction material, as did poured-concrete blocks. Before that, sand mortar was used. At 170 Prospect Terrace in Teaneck, a factory once stood that made ashlar concrete blocks.

Before 1895, Teaneck was a geographic railroad station name but did not exist as a municipality. From Cedar Lane north was part of Englewood Township. Englewood Township went from the Hudson to the Hackensack Rivers, between Cedar Lane and New Bridge Road. So West Englewood Avenue was the western section of Englewood Township. The street was built between 1873 and 1876 and owed its existence to a railroad station at 1400 Palisade Avenue (*see next page*).

West Englewood Railroad Station

In Teaneck, generally an east-west street was numbered by the address system put in service in 1922. On an east-west street, the address is the distance from the center line of Teaneck Road to the center line of the lot, divided by 10; so a house at 177 Englewood Avenue is 1,770 feet from the center line of Teaneck Road. For a north-south street, the address is the distance from the southernmost border of Teaneck extended, which as it turned out is the southern curb of Route 80 (not envisioned in the original plan); so, a building at 855 Windsor Road is 8,550 feet from the southern baseline. In most cases, the reason that a street is "east-west" is that it crosses Teaneck Road and has the same name, e.g., East Maple Street, East Cedar Lane, West Tryon Avenue. This designation does not apply to West Englewood Avenue.

Palisades Avenue was a commercial neighborhood from the 1870s. The block of West Englewood Avenue between Queen Anne Road and Palisade Avenue was about half occupied by commercial buildings by 1923, according to Sanborn (fire insurance) maps. This was developed long before Cedar Lane and had a post office, clothing store, shoe repair shop, stationery store, and hardware store. There was a railroad crossing here from 1873 to 1938. By 1926, the usefulness of the crossing was reduced, because the State Street bridge had been built.

In 1938, when children were returning from school, a beloved elderly man who sold vegetables and fruit from a horse-drawn truck was crossing the railroad tracks. Both he and the horse were deaf, and they were hit at speed by an express train. About three hundred children saw the man get decapitated and the horse badly injured. There was an outcry. The grade crossing was closed, and the pedestrian tunnel was built.

There was a West Englewood Post Office in 1873 but none in Teaneck until 1937. So the West Englewood Post Office delivered north of Cedar Lane; addresses south of it were serviced by Bogota or Leonia. Currently the West Englewood Post Office is a substation, but it was originally the main station that served most of Teaneck. The current one is the fourth location.

There had been a large, two-storey wood-frame railroad station where 1400 Palisade Avenue now stands. The railroad station was called the Jordan Station, after Conrad Jordan, a Teaneck resident who served as the Treasurer of the United States in the 1870s and then as an assistant secretary for the treasury in New York. It was an important site for freight and passenger service and mail. The building housed the post office and the railway express office for sending packages. North of it was a commercial development where coal and hay, feed, and grain were sold. It had a loading ramp where vehicles, horse-drawn and later motorized, could back up onto flat cars. This was a section control point on the railroad when it expanded in 1888.

When the railroad first started in 1873, there were only four trains a day, and there was no need for signaling. The few employees could be counted easily—whoever was not there was out on the road. Also, there was no need for sophisticated means to keep track of the trains—two went southbound in the morning, and two northbound in the afternoon. In the 1880s, the Ridgefield Park Railroad was bought by a company known as the Jersey City and Albany, which went bankrupt and was then bought by the West Shore Railroad. It went through the Weehawken tunnel under the Palisades and was extended to just south of Albany, where there were connections to Buffalo and points west. The railroad got to be a serious operation and went from one to three tracks. The signal station at West Englewood was staffed 24/7. The office was on the second floor, with a bay window and a telegraph key and railroad operator. The train dispatcher in Weehawken would send train orders by telegraph to the operator, who would operate manual (lantern) signals to stop trains or allow them to proceed. He would write out train orders on onion-skin paper and put them on a wand something like a jai-alai stick. A train man would pull it off as the train went past and read it to the conductor or engineer; then they would know whether to proceed to Dumont or stop at Haworth or another designated station. The Teaneck station at Cherry Lane came later, in the 1880s, and was just a neighborhood railroad station. So we had passenger rail service from 1873 to 1959.

Railroads were heavily regulated by the Interstate Commerce Commission and could not terminate passenger service without federal hearings. The railroad of that time was the New York Central, River Division. They decided to get rid of passenger service but could not do so directly. Since there was no federal control over their Weehawken-Manhattan ferry, however, that service was terminated and passengers thus had no way to get to New York. The ensuing dramatic drop in ridership in the 1950s enabled the railroad to get the feds to let them terminate the service as well.

Teaneck still has a healthy freight line, with forty-four trains a day, mostly containers bringing cargo from the Pacific coast, double-stacked, via Chicago. Some of these containers will be put on trucks in North Bergen or Elizabeth and delivered to local stores, and some will end up on other oceangoing vessels bound for Europe or Africa. These trains have a two-man crew. In the whole history of Teaneck, there have been only two train wrecks, two hazardous materials leaks, and a couple of fires in freight cars. Compared to the statistics of mishaps on Routes 80 and 95, that's pretty good.

The Plaza Commercial Neighborhood. Around 1900, developers started to build on the west side of the Teaneck tracks: on Windsor Road to Essex, from West Englewood to Warwick. Some of those buildings still exist, but the enterprise was an economic failure because there were no services other than the train station. The original developers, McCley and Davies, went out of business and sold it to two locals, Ayers and Lozier. Lozier was an old Dutch farm family, and Ayers' mother was one of the first female physicians in New Jersey, perhaps the first. These two men had money and a better understanding of business; so, around 1917, after analyzing the reasons for the original failure, they chose to set up northern Queen Anne Road as a Teaneck business district.

Ayers Court was originally Market Street, so named with the obvious idea of establishing markets on it for the commuters getting off the train. The building at 1407 Palisade to 210 Plaza, one of the first commercial ones, dates from about 1917. It had a few unique features. Cast-iron stars dress up the façade about twelve feet from the ground. These stars are decorative washers on the ends of rods that go through the building from front to back to counteract the outward thrust of the structure.

Unfortunately, the land on which it was constructed was sandy and swampy. The builder used a steam-powered excavator at the edge of the ditch, which went down about eight to ten feet, without shoring. The vibration of the excavator caused the side of the ditch to collapse and the machine to fall in. The operator was injured, and the machine had to be dismantled to get it back to the street. That excavator was probably the biggest machine in Bergen County at the time.

People who bought houses included those from different ethnic groups who wanted to fit in and, perhaps, fancied themselves as British landed gentry, so many streets have English historical names, e.g., Warwick, Essex, Maitland, Rutland, Windsor, and so forth.

State Street was intended as a visual gateway to the housing development on the other side of the tracks. After erecting the State Street Bridge, the developers got permission from the railroad and the township to use it as a public bridge. State Street was to be an extra-wide funnel to the real estate office at 258 West Englewood Avenue, to draw in house buyers.

The Ackerman farm, where black angora goats were raised, once stood at 1500 Teaneck Road. They had a huge barn, which lasted into the 1950s.

The building at 34 State Street (*see next page*) won an architectural award in 1929, was featured on the cover of *Architecture Digest* (Journal of the American Institute of Architects), and was voted the best of the year at a time when a great many apartments were being built all over the country. The developer had intended to erect eight five-storey apartment buildings, but the Depression prevented the rest of the project from going forward. This was Teaneck's first fire-resistant apartment house (most others have wooden joists), and it probably contains

34 State Street

the first apartment elevator as well.

On May 24, 1942, two planes collided over Teaneck and State. (See beginning of "Central Teaneck" walk.) A mom-and-pop bus barn stood at 1425 Teaneck Road from about 1912; it ran a small fleet of buses (ten or twelve), driven by family members, that went from Hackensack to Dumont. One of its main features was that it was a feeder for the DeGraw Avenue trolley line.

The neighborhood east of Beveridge Street was laid out right after World War I. The local VFW chapter influenced a lot of street names to commemorate local heroes of that war. Schoonmaker Road was named after Captain Stephen T. Schoonmaker, who served with the 101st Infantry Regiment, 26th Infantry Division, and was posthumously awarded the Distinguished Service Cross in the battle of the Argonne forest, the October 1918 campaign that effectively ended the war. It had been essentially the last chance for the Germans to win.

Schoonmaker was an infantry company commander who had lived with his father on River Road when the war started, and had enlisted. He went to Officers' Candidate School and ended up in a New England outfit—the 101st is the old 1st Massachusetts, which was first organized in the seventeenth century. His unit was pinned down by a German machine gun nest in a well-defined defensive position complete with concrete bunkers and telephone communications. Schoonmaker led by example. He rushed the emplacement, wiped out the machine guns, and was killed.

A lot of local guys were in the 78th Division—the Jersey Lightning—and most of the other street names were after them.

At the end of Schoonmaker is Hubert Terrace, named after Sergeant Hubert T. Roch of the 308th Infantry in the Argonne. In Teaneck, we have a large park named Argonne, as well as Argonne Court, both in commemoration of the offensive in northeast France, north of Sedan in 1918. Another street, Basil Street, which commemorated Private Basil Smith, who also died in the Argonne, was eliminated when Argonne Park was expanded.

Beveridge Street was named after Private First Class Wallage T. Beveridge, U.S. Army Medical Corps. He had been a medic but never made it overseas since he was injured in a training accident in Tennessee, while the army was getting ready. When he left the army, he became a doctor, came back to Teaneck, and started the veterans' movement here.

Two streets elsewhere in Teaneck were named after heroic fire fighters—Farrant Terrance for Floyd Farrant, who lost his sight trying to rescue a woman at a house fire at DeGraw and Hickory; and Dohrman Avenue after Henry K. Dohrman, badly injured in a construction fire at Holy Name Hospital in 1926.

The parking lot at Beveridge Street and Teaneck Road was supposed to have been the location of a police precinct. At first, Teaneck was going to have one police headquarters and two precincts—one here, and the other at the municipal lot at Beverly and Teaneck; however, this need was eliminated when police cars got two-way radios.

What is now West Gate Road was the site of Conrad N. Jordan's mansion. He had been a successful Wall Street executive who became Treasurer of the United States and was so well liked, honest, and effective that he was asked to stay as the assistant treasurer. Eventually he got to be in charge of the sub-treasury at Wall and Broad Streets in New York. His land extended from Teaneck Road to the railroad. The original West Englewood railroad station was the Jordan Station. He used to commute from there to the New York ferry in Weehawken. One winter evening on his return trip, as the ferry was starting to pull out of the dock, a woman from West Orange, realizing that she was going to miss it, ran toward the ferry, jumped and missed, and fell into the river. Jordan took off his overcoat, dove into the water, rescued the woman, and gave her the coat.

For this he received the Carnegie Medal, which is awarded every year to brave citizens. The medal came with a $1,000.00 prize, which Jordan contributed to the woman's favorite charity.

If we had been at West Englewood and Teaneck Road in the 19th century, on the northwest corner we would have seen the office of Dr. Mary Ayres, one of the first female physicians in New Jersey.

The apartment house at 17 West Englewood Avenue was built in 1929. By that time Jordan's mansion was derelict and the neighborhood was changing. Some of Teaneck's firemen had gone at their own expense to the New Haven City Fire Training Center, which was then one of the few like it, and learned how to deal with apartment house fires. On the night of January 30, 1930, someone set fire to the Jordan mansion, probably in an act of vandalism. The firemen, who had been specially trained, saved the adjoining apartment building.

On the southwest corner of West Englewood and Teaneck Road stands a "taxpayer" building from 1925, so-called because land had been bought on speculation with the purpose of erecting a cheap row of stores, enough to pay the taxes until an apartment building could be put up. As it turned out, the stores were worth enough in themselves.

Teaneck Club, 1304 Teaneck Road

Now a four-family apartment house, 1304 Teaneck Road was the Teaneck Club in the late 19th and early 20th centuries. It was a private recreational building housing Teaneck's first movie theater and first bowling alley, and had a dance floor. At one time it was called "the Raven" because, when they made it a movie theater, they painted the windows black but then decided that did not look very appealing and painted the whole thing black. This was in the 1880s to 1920s.

The First Presbyterian Church of Teaneck (at Church Street and Teaneck Road) is the oldest continuous-use religious building in the township. The Lenapes had a long house for their native religion at Lindbergh and George for hundreds, possibly thousands, of years. A Lutheran church stood at River and Rutland from 1702 to just after the Revolutionary War. But their members had been loyalists during the war, and if they wanted to stay alive, they had to leave. The building was abandoned and burned down in a 1820 grass fire.

The predecessor of the current Presbyterian Church was the Washington Avenue Union Sunday school, from the 1880s. Teaneck Road from Cedar Lane north was Washington Avenue as part of Englewood Township. It was a "Union" Sunday school because people of all Protestant denominations could belong to it. In 1841, a Presbyterian church, at 1187 Teaneck Road, started in a public school. They eventually moved to 1 Church Street and became the current Teaneck Presbyterian Church.

The vacant lot at Church Street and Teaneck Road was the site of Teaneck's first municipal building. From 1895 to 1907, there was no municipal building. The mayor would hold meetings in his house or arrange for some other place.

There was an 1869 school building where the Teaneck Ignition Service now stands at 1188 Teaneck Road; the school became surplus in 1907 when the school moved to 1 West Forest, a building that was recently torn down as the Townhouse, which had served from 1907 to 1940 was an elementary school. This freed up the 1869 building, which was moved from 1188 Teaneck Road to 1234 Teaneck Road. In 1926, it was superseded by the current municipal building. That building got moved again to Mackle Park and became the VFW headquarters until in the 1950s, when it was torn down.

It was very common in the 19th century to move buildings. There were no overhead wires, few underground utilities, and land was dirt cheap.

This is Fire Headquarters, which was built in 1948. It's the fourth fire station in this neighborhood. At the time it was built, it had the largest apparatus floor without columns in the country. The architect was Milton Cady—a descendant of Elizabeth Cady Stanton—who was noted for designing in the Georgian style, like the municipal building, the old police station, and fire headquarters.

Fire Station and Public School, 1904

The first fire station in this neighborhood stood at 1188 Teaneck Road. It was a nice building, painted white and owned by Walter Selvage. He leased it for a minimal payment to the volunteer fire department to protect his new development; however, he was not an easy guy to get along with and would not allow the members to occupy the quarters unless there was official business or an alarm. They could not socialize, have access to their lockers, or check their gear. After about three years of that, they got their own station.

In 1907, the firefighters in that station purchased the land now occupied by 14-18 Fairview Avenue—a four-family house. They built a foundation. After buying a barn on Lafayette Place in Englewood, they rented twenty mules with harness, cut a corduroy road through the forest that is now Argonne Park, dragged the barn over, parked it on the foundation, and made it a fire station. It became fire headquarters in 1915 and stayed that way until 1920. It housed a hand-drawn hose reel and a ladder truck that could be drawn by people or horses.

In Teaneck, there were forty-six fire gongs, which were made out of locomotive wheels suspended on a kind of gallows framework with a hammer and an enamel sign that indicated what number to strike. So if you were at the fire gong at Teaneck Road and Forest Avenue, you would have to strike "12", i.e., one stroke, then two, and other people would go to the fire gong near them and relay the number. The fire fighters then came to the station and took the hand-drawn hose wagon to the scene. There were three horse teams trained to take the ladder—the milk, ice, and U.S. mail teams.

The first team to hook up to the ladder truck would get the run and receive fifty cents. The horses were paid on call; the men were not. In 1907, just after this station was built, William Walter Phelps' widow gave a touring car to the fire company. They painted it red and took out the back seat. They also modified the hand-drawn hose reel so that it could be mounted on the back of the car and drop hose off while driving down the street; or, by using levers, the reel could be dismounted and pulled by hand. This was a German-style hose reel called a Dividor.

By 1915, the township was willing to take responsibility for fire protection. Before that, there were five independent companies in different neighborhoods. The township approached them with the prospect of a municipal fire department that would maintain the stations and grant authority but not pay. Four of the five companies agreed and, depending on the dates of their founding, were numbered. Fourteen Fairview Avenue became Company #1 and also headquarters. The building was, however, inadequate for motor apparatus, so

Teaneck Fire Headquarters, c. 1920

a new headquarters at 1213 Teaneck Road was built in 1920.

It had a four-storey tower— useful for drying hose and as a training tower. The back bay did not exist—in fact, it was a two-bay house. In 1930, a third bay was added. If you notice, the fire company name is on the front of the building, which is now a commercial building.

St. Anastasia's Church. The original St. Anastasia's Church (*see next page*) dates to 1907 and served as such until a new church was built across the street in 1936. This was a bit unusual for several reasons. There weren't many Catholics in Teaneck until the 1920s, and there was a lot of prejudice against them, especially against the Irish and Italians. Walter Selvage was a rarity in that he was a wealthy Catholic. His wife, née Anastasia Kelly, named the church after her

The Original St. Anastasia's Church, 1907

patron saint. They brought in Carmelite priests who had a parish in Bogota.

In the 1920s, there was an active Ku Klux Klan unit based in Teaneck's Glenwood Park section. They persecuted Catholics and wanted to prevent Al Smith from being elected President of the United States in 1928. Eventually, however, more and more Catholics moved into the area.

If we were on Teaneck Road in the 19th and early 20th centuries, its appearance would have been much different from what we see today. To begin with, there was no Route 4 until 1929–32. Teaneck was lined with mansions, containing an average of eighteen rooms, all the way from Fort Lee Road to Bergenfield. Most houses had live-in servants. Preferred servants were black, as they tended to be Protestant and Americans; the Irish were a second choice.

A large Italian neighborhood also existed in Teaneck, bordered by Amsterdam, Shepherd, and Tryon Avenues and Washington Place. People would come over from the old country as an entire village and settle here. Most immigrant groups had a society to help the newcomers to find jobs and housing. Many Italian men started farms; some went into the construction industry, trucking, moving, and trash collection. Italian women became seamstresses. A big sweatshop at Teaneck Road and Elizabeth Avenue, called the Rosemaid Corporation, manufactured hand-sewn slippers. It was a real firetrap and had poor lighting. The Teaneck Fire Department would show up there on Sunday and drill over and over on the building, since they assumed there would be a repetition of the dreadful New York Triangle Shirtwaist fire some day. Luckily, that never happened, and when Route 4 was constructed, the sweatshop was demolished. Across the river in Hackensack, Goldberg's Slipper Company—which also hired young women—had sprinklers and sanitary facilities for the employees. This historian lived across the street from a woman who had worked, first for Rosemaid, and then Goldberg's, and who said there was a major difference.

The central section of the commercial building at 961 Teaneck Road is actually an old Dutch farm house, which still contains slave shackles. Slavery existed in New Jersey until July 4, 1804. Anyone born in or entering the state after that date was no longer a slave, but there was a forty-year grace period for the purpose of preventing older slaves—a seventy-year-old black man in poor health, say—from being summarily dismissed by the owner. The front section is from the 1960s, and other apartments from the 1930s.

The building at 927 Commonwealth Drive is very unusual. It was

Teaneck's First Condo, 927 Commonwealth Drive

one of the first condominiums in Teaneck, converted in the 1930s. It was originally built as a mansion for a Civil War hero, Walter Coe, who lived here after the war, when Phelps invited other wealthy people to come to Teaneck. Coe had two teenage sons who played musical instruments at the Teaneck Club. They were walking home one night past the school building at Teaneck and Forest Avenue when they saw a candle light and a man trying to steal money from the teacher's desk. At the time there was no township police or even a township. There was the Englewood Township Protective Society, a part-paid, part-volunteer police force headquartered where the Bergen PAC theater now stands. One of the boys ran down Forest Avenue and got the police to respond. His brother hid in the bushes until the robber emerged and confronted him. The felon pistol-whipped the boy in the head, but he fought back, injuring the robber. There were no ambulances or hospitals. The Coe boy was taken home and gave a good description of the robber. The only quick regional means of communication was the railroad telegraph, so the police used it to broadcast the description. As it turned out, the man showed up in Jersey City and went to the railroad hospital (common in the 19th century, when they were maintained by the various railroads in Jersey City to treat injured employees). He tried to claim that he was a train employee who had fallen off a car, and he was thus caught by the railroad police.

Coe moved from Teaneck to Englewood Cliffs and became its first mayor, with a large mansion on Sylvan Avenue. His Teaneck house thus became available and was purchased by Bernard Lippmann, one of the first Jewish people in Teaneck. He was accepted because he was a powerful, influential Wall Street lawyer. He and his wife took an interest in the board of education and the public library. Mrs. Lippmann got the library moved out of a former slave cabin at 1261 Teaneck Road to its current location at 840 Teaneck Road. They had a synagogue in 1933 at the Teaneck Jewish Community Center on Manor Court. When the Lippmanns moved out, 927 Commonwealth became a Masonic lodge called the Circle in the Square, which operated until the Depression, when the members could no longer afford the dues. The building was sold for taxes and so became a condominium in about 1937, which, as previously noted, was rare for the time.

Probably the most prominent feature in northeast Teaneck is currently occupied by the National Guard Armory (*see next page*). The armory itself was built in 1937 for the purpose of replacing smaller neighborhood armories in adjoining towns. It was the home of the 113th Infantry and 104th Engineers, and is now the home of 250th Brigade Support Battalion.

During World War II, the armory was a full-time military installation and served as the first stop for local draftees. The triangle of

Teaneck Armory

land the building occupies, together with some adjoining properties, previously housed the tri-town poor farm, a social welfare facility that provided housing and work opportunities for those who could not support themselves. A city directory from 1900 lists some of the inhabitants as "drug addict," "alcoholic," and "consumptive." Tubercular clients lived in a row of cottages and worked to the extent of their ability tending cows, chickens, and large vegetable plots. The farm had initially been operated, not by Teaneck, but by Palisades, Englewood, and Ridgefield townships.

In the 1920s, Bergen Pines in Paramus was established to take care of those with long-term health problems, such as tuberculosis. Others who could not support themselves received cash from the state—"home relief"—and the farm thus became superfluous.

The property on the north is Liberty Road, which is an 18th-century street that cut diagonally from Liberty Pole monument in Englewood toward New Bridge Road. This was an important part of the retreat route of the American revolutionaries from the Fort Lee garrison on November 20, 1776.

Across from the Armory are four residential side streets that run between Teaneck Road and the railroad. In the 19th century, that land belonged to Samuel Tilden, a prominent New York state politician. At some point, he deeded the land to the New York City Public Library, and what is now Armory Place was originally going to be named Library Place. The current houses on these blocks were constructed just after World War II. Before that, almost the whole area was occupied by the Hannibal Coal Company, a large distributor of coal for heating and cooking. The 1700 block of Palisade Avenue used to be called Siding Road because of the railroad siding that allowed delivery of coal and later of propane. Subsequently, the property became subdivided for houses, leaving a small facility operated by Suburban Fuel. By the 1970s, it was replaced by the current spice factory.

The residential blocks that run east from Teaneck Road between Ward Plaza and Tryon Avenue all look as if they were built at the same time; however, Voorhees Street is much older than its neighbors and is shown on the 1903 street map. The other streets did not appear until after 1922. Ward Plaza is different, because it is very wide and was built this way in order to serve as an assembly area for four columns of army trucks, called "serials," formed up in case the unit stationed at the Armory had to deploy. Until the 1970s, when the National Guard went for summer training, they would march from Ward Plaza to the West Englewood railroad station, led by a band. The townspeople would cheer as they boarded a troop train taking them to Camp Drum, NY. Traditionally, the band would play the march "The Girl I Left Behind Me".

The area along the railroad tracks in the vicinity of State Street has a long commercial history. In the 1880s, the West Englewood rail station was upgraded so that it could be staffed 24/7 with a telegraph operator to help control train traffic. The station was a focus for local residents because of the Western Union and Railway Express agencies—predecessors of UPS, FedEx, and others. North of the station stood a water tank for refilling steam locomotive tenders, and a rail siding with a so-called "circus" ramp for loading and unloading wheeled vehicles from the flat cars. A fuel and feed business developed along that siding. Eventually, large wooden coal bunkers were built across the street and the railroad track led in to facilitate bulk delivery of coal. Horse-drawn wagons would then be fed by gravity from the coal pocket for local deliveries. In 1930, the coal pocket collapsed and was replaced by a series of four hundred-foot-tall concrete silos fed by conveyor machinery that still used the gravity method of filling delivery vehicles, which by then were all motorized.

In the 19th century, a doctor developed a sanatorium complex—another alternative for people with chronic health problems who were unable to care for themselves. After several name changes, the complex came to be called the Nelden Sanatorium. The main building stretched along Nelden Road. On the flat land just east of it, which is now part of Argonne Park, sat several small cottages and a farm that helped support, and give work to, the patients. The complex became vacant in the early 1940s.

4

Southeast Teaneck

SOUTHEAST TEANECK

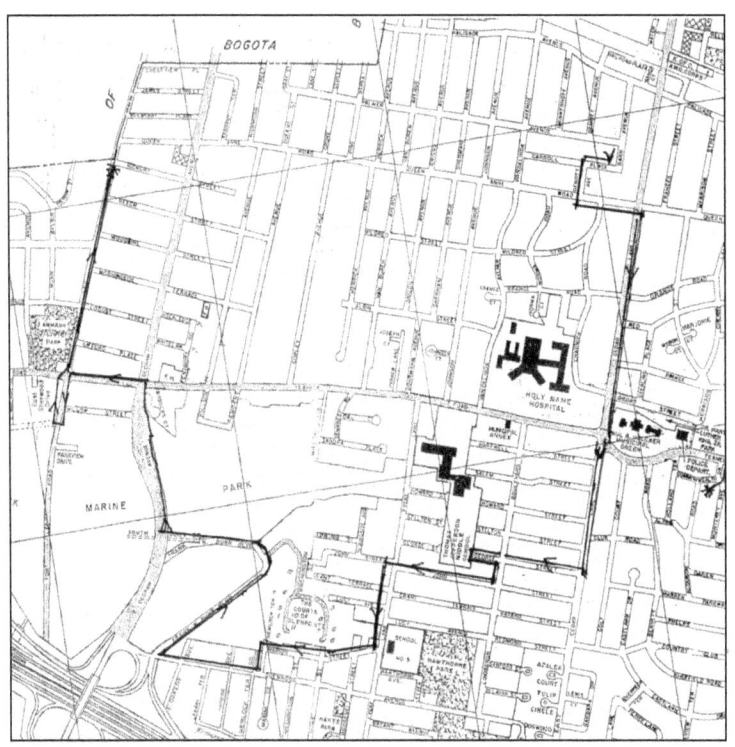

Southeast Teaneck Walk Map

A T CARROLL PLACE AND BARR AVENUE stood the Fiss, Doerr, and Carroll horse stables with a large main building—a hundred by three hundred feet—and some outbuildings.

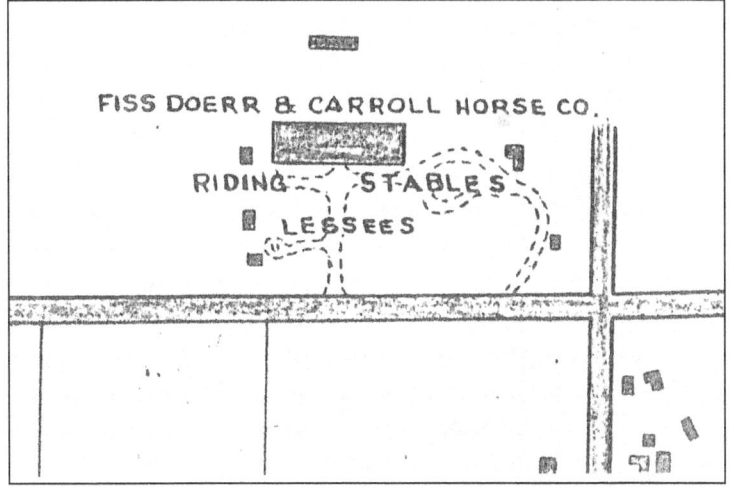

The Fiss, Doerr, and Carroll Horse Company, from a 1912 map

They bought horses from various farmers and trained them for specific jobs. One major contract was for several local transit companies that operated horse-drawn street cars in Newark and Jersey City. They also acted as a leasing stable for people who did not own a horse or wanted to have one for a weekend or an event. Probably the crowning glory of the stables was their supplying horses to the French and Imperial Russian armies in World War I. Those horses were marched across the Cedar Lane grade crossing (there was no bridge at that time) and loaded onto railcars for shipment to the docks in Hoboken. The stables constituted Teaneck's biggest commercial enterprise before

World War I. The township then was comprised of only about eight hundred people. As motor vehicles supplanted horses, the facility became vacant. In 1919, a spectacular nighttime arson fire wiped out the empty buildings. The fire department was hampered due to a lack of pumping apparatus, as this is a very high spot, the water that came out of the hydrants did not have sufficient pressure behind it.

In 1926, Cedar Lane was widened, and another very steep hill (between Chestnut and Elm) was reduced as part of the project to lower the grade of the railroad and a build a bridge to bring Cedar Lane over the tracks.

Bohne's Dairy

In 1900, behind the gas station at 209 Cedar Lane, we would have seen ten or eleven barns and other agricultural buildings belonging to the Phelps estate. The area north of Cedar between Teaneck Road and the railroad tracks was essentially the heart of the property, inasmuch as it was a working dairy and grain farm. The last barn there (Bohne's) was still being used as a dairy-distribution facility in 1961. This was one of the few sites on Cedar Lane with commercial activity around the turn of the 20th century. Another business was a family-owned fish and vegetable stand where Cedar crosses the Hackensack River. A gift shop at Pomander and Cedar also existed. Seven gasoline-powered street lights, which functioned much like Coleman lanterns (a gasoline lamp used in camping) provided the only illumination on Cedar Lane from the river to the Overpeck Creek. You can imagine how effective that was.

Local tradition puts the site of Phelps' grange (a threshing barn where wheat is separated from chaff) on the southwest corner of Merrison and Grange. Grange Road was one of Phelps' riding streets. As a private property owner, he developed an extensive street network, most of which has been obliterated. On occasion, people planting a garden will dig down and find a catch basin or piece of a curb in an odd place. This was part of the road system that was abandoned when the bulk of the Phelps estate was broken up between 1922 and 1926. Grange Road is a segment of one of his private roadways and is named either after the actual threshing floor or for his mansion, which was called "the Grange". Before that it was the Henry J. Brinkerhoff farm—a working farm that was not part of a large estate.

Red Road also follows a private riding street that went up past the high school athletic field and diverged onto River Road south of Phelps' son's house in the vicinity of River Road and Ramapo. The area contained large woodlands. Red Road acquired its name because all the buildings on the estate were painted dark red. The original road contained a row of workers' houses, which were part of their wages. Some of these houses still exist today along the south side of Bennett Road in the 30s and 50s addresses. They were moved there in 1906 by Mrs. Phelps (Mr. Phelps was dead by that time) because she wanted the land for some other purpose. Bennett Road was named after the superintendent or manager of the estate.

Phelps had huge stables roughly on the site of the Jewish Community Center (Prince Street). These were nicer than the average person's house in the quality of their woodwork, stonework, and ironwork. Fitted with mansard roofs and cedar shingles, they were quite expensive. They were the subject of an arson fire in 1888.

Where did the Phelps's get their money? William Walter Phelps' father founded the Delaware Lackawanna and Western railroad. The earlier Phelps's had been farmers and miners in Connecticut and Pennsylvania. Phelps the elder started the railroad to bring coal into the area, from Scranton into New York Harbor, and thereby made a great deal of money. His son was sent to Yale and became a lawyer in the era just before the Civil War, when the economy was revolutionized and real estate deals abounded. The family made even more money, and William Walter Phelps was like a baron, though certainly not of the robber variety. He was very generous. When a bank in Hackensack that he had nothing to do with failed due to embezzlement, Phelps paid all the bank depositors with less than three thousand dollars on deposit— basically rescuing many working-class families who could ill afford to lose their life savings. He was similarly philanthropic when disease broke out.

The intersection of Cedar Lane and Teaneck Road is a significant one. The Lenapes laid out the original pathways for Cedar Lane, Teaneck Road, New Bridge Road, River Road, and possibly Fort Lee Road, although this last is in dispute. They had a good eye for what they were doing, because good drainage probably made these roads available for use when other areas of the township were sunk in mud for half the year. Cedar Lane was an important municipal boundary from 1869 to 1895. The center line of Cedar was the dividing line between Englewood and Ridgefield Townships. Below Cedar Lane (or Cedar Lane Road, as it was called on maps then) was Teaneck Road. Above Cedar from the present numbering system of 800 and up, it was Washington Avenue—a name it retains in Bergenfield and Dumont.

The municipal green was the original site of the farm of Henry J. Brinkerhoff, whose family had lived had lived there for two hundred years prior to 1865. He had originally bought the land from the heirs of Sarah Kierstadt, who had been given all of Teaneck and Bogota by the Lenapes in gratitude for a translation job that enabled Chief Oratam to straighten out deed disputes with the Dutch. A lot of misunderstandings occurred because the Lenapes thought they were selling (or, more properly, "renting") fishing and hunting rights that could not be passed on to heirs. People killed each other over such disputes.

The Kierstadt property was eventually broken up into the farms that were here in the 18th century and a bit into the 19th. When Phelps came, there was a big house at 818 Teaneck Road that had belonged to Brinkerhoff. It was enlarged to three hundred feet in length and about seventy-five wide, one- and two-storey. Phelps made it look like a chalet and filled it with expensive artwork. He had taken trips all over the world, both as a government official and private citizen, and brought back the art and sculpture from Europe. He equipped the house with gaslight. There were no public gas pipes yet, so in the 1880s, he installed a generating plant in the basement. It looked something like a boiler, in which calcium carbide and water—mixed by the house crew—would generate acetylene gas, which traveled through pipes to fixtures that could be turned on and off as needed.

On the evening of March 31, 1888, however, someone made a big mistake. The practice was to stop generating the acetylene about two or three hours before bedtime, let the gas burn off, then turn off the jets. They missed the fixture in the picture gallery, which was a two-storey room with a balcony—a perfect setup for a fire. The following night, April 1, when the generator was started, the gas came out unburned from the open jet and filled up the room. The family noticed the garlic-like smell and notified Mr. Bennett, the manager, who lived next door, where the police station is now. When he opened the door to the gallery, the gas flowed out into the hall in an explosive concentration. It was probably too rich to explode in the gallery but, when mixed with the air in the hallway, it encountered a flame of some kind and blew up. There was no Teaneck Fire Department because there was no Teaneck. The Hackensack Fire Department was not obligated to respond—Englewood was. A rider was sent from the estate to pull the fire alarm box in Hackensack near where Sears is now, and another to go to fire headquarters on Van Brunt Street (where the theater now stands) in Englewood. Both agencies responded, but by the time they got there, either with hand or horse-drawn vehicles, the building was pretty much gone. The neighbors had saved much of the artwork and personal effects and put them in the stables, which were also in danger of burning—the shingles had started to smoke. The Hackensack Fire Department took draught from a mill pond where Thomas Jefferson Middle School is located, and relay-pumped it up to the house. A Hackensack fireman went up a ladder and used an ax to knock off burning shingles while waiting for the water, but he over-reached and fell off. He was seriously injured, but he did save the stables. From then until the 1920s, the mansion remained a ruin. Ivy grew over the brickwork. Very little else was left of the structure. It was referred to as the "ruins", and people would come to have their pictures taken by it.

Phelps, at the time a U.S. congressman, had been notified by telegram. After determining that his family was all right, he walked across the street to a mansion owned by C.R. Griggs, a cotton dealer. It is now the location of Holy Name Hospital. Phelps negotiated the price, whipped out a roll of bills, bought the house, and moved his family across the street. The house fire was accidental, but the stables were arsoned a couple of months later. No horses were lost, but all of the harnesses and carriages burned.

That's not the only thing that happened here. On the hospital lawn, a marker commemorates the encampment of the Continental Army in the summer of 1780. It included three regiments of regular army infantry, called Continentals, who were full-time soldiers with an enlistment contract. They were stationed here in tents, operated against the British army in the present Hudson County and along the Palisades, and were getting ready to drive the British out of New York. In this part of their campaign, and for the only time, the Bergen County militia fought in line of battle like European soldiers. The Bergen and Orange militias drove British forces out of Fort Lee in the summer of 1780—a fact that is not well known. Their professional abilities had advanced considerably in the four years since the British took the fort.

In 1903, a law changed the name from "militia" to "National Guard" in honor of the 71st Regiment of New York militia, which was the ideal model due to their tactical and logistical skills. The change was due to a War Department study of the weak points of the American army during the Spanish-American war. It was found that the individual soldiers from militia units performed well, but that their officers were not used to handling more than thirty to fifty men. During that war, thousands died because they lacked basic skills such as cleaning a field kitchen or digging latrines downstream from the water supply. The 1903 law required large-unit drills of regimental-sized (about fifteen hundred men) formations once a year; however, it did not provide for training bases, like Fort Dix, which meant using large public or private parks instead. The local National Guard decided to hold a large-scale battle drill through Teaneck on Memorial Day 1906. They met with the widow Phelps, who was not using the estate by then, and got approval for its use. National Guard battalions from Paterson and Newark—having come up by streetcar—met where Sears is now. The battalion from Bergen County was told to defend the Englewood Armory against this force. The "battle" was umpired by captains from West Point. The Bergen County battalion was supposed to have been assisted by the 2nd New Jersey Cavalry, from Jersey City, but that unit had already been committed to a ceremony for the holiday. They rented some cars, mounted machine guns on them, and within a few hours assembled the first mechanized cavalry, eight years before any of the world's other armies.

The defender had an official U.S. government map. The invaders had a private-sector street map. The first contact was made on the Linden Avenue hill of Cedar Lane. The defending mechanized cavalry razzle-dazzled a bit and fell back to near Teaneck Road. Along the ridge east of Teaneck Road, infantry and artillery were dug in. The scouts for the invaders got there and realized that they were not going to just go east on Cedar Lane, turn left, and get to Englewood. So they examined the real map (not the government one) and saw that Cherry Lane existed. The main invaders turned left on Palisade, right on Cherry Lane, and then outflanked the main defensive position. Part of the invading battalions of infantry slipped through the woods and found another street on the real map, Genessee Avenue, which was then called Glade Road. They slipped in behind the Englewood defenses, established all around Forest and Lafayette

Avenue, and captured the Englewood armory by 11:00 in the morning. The exercise was supposed to last until 3:00, but everyone had an early lunch.

It was a worthwhile exercise and probably saved the lives of the men who later served in World War I. The privates and lieutenants later became the senior sergeants and colonels for elements of the 79th Infantry, the 42nd Infantry, or other outfits that came from the area.

The Volks Funeral Home was the site of the home of General van Buren, who had served as a light infantry brigadier general from New York State during the Civil War. After the war, he acquired the land and built a house on the site of Volks. He had a daughter who was ahead of her time in her willingness to travel unescorted in Europe. While there, she met a man who presented himself as the Count di Castelmenardo. He was a good actor but not an aristocrat. After she married him and expressed a desire to see his ancestral home in Italy, she found out that the count was of no account, but she kept the title and returned to Teaneck. When she got too old to maintain her house, around 1912, she sold it to a business that opened the Blue Bird Inn, a nice roadhouse-type restaurant with a liquor license. In 1919, when Prohibition made that illegal, they got rid of the license but not the liquor. In other words, the place became a speakeasy.

On the corner of Golf Court and Teaneck Road stood a place called the Palm Gardens (*see next page*), which was a combination bowling alley, dance hall, and restaurant—also a speakeasy. The owners of the Blue Bird Inn imported some gangsters from Hudson County to help them compete with the Palm Gardens, bought land on the southwest corner of Cedar Lane and Teaneck Road, and put up the Blue Bird Inn Dance Hall. The Palm Gardens won out in the ensuing competition, so the Blue Bird Inn decided to collect its fire insurance. One of the

Former Palm Gardens

gangsters came up the idea of using chicken stomachs as incendiary devices. They tied off the lower end of each stomach with string, filled the stomachs with small quantities with gasoline, and draped the upper parts around light bulbs. When the lights came on, eventually they burst and sprayed burning gasoline onto the contents of the dance hall. The technique was only partly successful, however, since the fire investigators found some unexploded gizzards. The arsonist was thus caught.

The building at 885 Teaneck Road had been a bowling alley and, before that, a car dealership in the 1930s. This was the original site of Phelps' greenhouse, which he began as a hobby but which was later developed into a commercial enterprise by his son, John J. Phelps, who grew tulips and other flowers out of season to supply to restaurants and hotels. The greenhouse building was not removed until the 1930s.

East Cedar Lane used to be a through street to Englewood. It was first created by the Lenapes. The Overpeck Creek was shallow water that was later dug out for Englewood flood control in 1894. This was what led indirectly to the establishment of Teaneck. Farmers who lived in West Englewood did not benefit from the canal but paid a hundred percent more taxes. They joined with people who similarly lacked services and, by a vote in February 1895, created the township of Teaneck. The site, before the canal, was built along a shallow creek that ran rapidly during rain. A small mill was here before the Revolution. This area was used as one of the escape routes by the American army surrounded in Fort Lee. In 1776, the soldiers forded the creek, came down Cedar Lane to River Road, and were rescued by the Massachusetts state marines, who ferried them to the main body of the army in Hackensack. The area remained mostly open through the 1930s and contained one of the last farms—the Lewis farm. The Association of Sanitary Contractors eventually purchased the land as a garbage dump.

Teaneck's original inhabitants were the Lenni-Lenapes whom Europeans called the Delawares. The local branch that lived in Teaneck were the Hackensackii, who owned a large portion of Bergen County.

The permanent Lenape settlements were located along Lindbergh Boulevard. One village had about a hundred houses and a religious/municipal building called a long house. There were also two suburbs, or subsidiary hamlets—near Lindbergh and Glenwood (that is, near the little league field), and near East Cedar.

The Lenapes built on high ground so as to avoid problems with swamp-borne diseases and for observation. They were peaceful people who grew crops and medicinal herbs, had strong family and religious ties, and desired to get along with their neighbors. Not all other native peoples had the same attitude. There was a long-term conflict between the Mohicans and the Delawares. Just prior to the arrival of the Europeans, the Iroquois beat the Mohicans in battle and forced them to sign a treaty to pay taxes. Wood Ridge was a military garrison of the Mohicans, who were locally called Moonachies. They patrolled this area to make sure the taxes were paid, rather like revenue police. The Hackensackii also sought protection against the Tappan Indians and built a fort where Brett Park now stands, on Riverview Avenue between River and New Bridge Roads. There is a bend in the Hackensack River with a bluff. The fort was on this bluff and served to protect the community from fishing incursions by Tappan river canoes. Before the advent of wheeled vehicles, canoes afforded the most convenient mode of transportation. Excavations over the years have turned up many arrowheads and spearheads from their in-ground armory. At that time, the Dutch were not interested in oppressing the local people. Quite the contrary—they wanted to trade manufactured goods for furs, especially beaver pelts, which were very popular in Europe. Beavers were very plentiful, and the Lenapes had developed the skill to trap them and to cure the hides.

The first European activities occurred at the corner of River and Fort Lee Roads in Bogota, where the Winkelmann family had a trading post. Beaver pelts would be traded for knives (the Lenapes did not have iron-working skills), guns, alcohol, and clothes. At first, the relationship between Europeans and Indians was cordial. The attitude of the Dutch company that ran New Netherlands (New York–New Jersey colonies) changed when they decided to settle people here. They did not, however, want to seize land but to negotiate and pay for it, but there was a fundamental difference in the concept of land ownership between the natives and the Europeans. To the Lenape, property rights involved the communal use of the land to hunt and fish, but they could not be transferred to heirs or resold. The Europeans' view held land ownership to mean ownership by a family that could be passed on, sold, and even lost for non-payment of taxes.

There was no easy way to translate the differing ideas before Sarah Kierstadt, who developed a Dutch/Lenape dictionary.

Not everyone, moreover, dealt fairly, and some Dutch discovered that giving alcohol to the Lenape before negotiations made things go better for the Europeans. Eventually the Dutch governor, Kieft—a crooked politician who wanted to rob everyone—touched off a war between the Europeans and the native people.

Kieft was removed, and Peter Stuyvesant became governor. He had the mind of a businessman, sought out Lenape leaders, and found Oratam—or Oritani—a native sachem or judge. He tasked the Indian leader with the additional duties of deputy sheriff, and because of his dual offices Oratam had the right to arrest both Lenapes and Dutch. He enforced prohibition laws for real estate negotiations and standard contracts. He lived into his nineties.

Some Lenapes intermarried with Europeans. The last tribal settlement, until the 1930s, was at 505 Main Street in Hackensack, behind Holy Trinity Roman Catholic Church. Most local Lenapes moved voluntarily in 1760 to the first Indian reservation, in Burlington County. The Lenapes asked for land so that they could continue their tribal life. This probably would have worked, except that Quakers coming from Philadelphia wanted the land as well.

The two movie houses that existed in Hackensack for many decades, the Fox and the Oritani, were both named for the Lenapes. Fox was the last of their local chiefs, and lived here in the 1930s.

Before Thomas Jefferson Middle School was built in 1958–1959, the athletic field was a U.S. army air defense artillery post for a battery of 90-mm radar-guided anti-aircraft cannon. Howard, Stelton, and

George Streets ended at what is now the sides of the school field. During the Korean War, the army built a series of "streets" with roofs of buildings that would be there if it were really a residential neighborhood as seen from the air. These "streets" connected existing dead ends of actual residential streets but the eaves of the roofs were at ground level and concealed mountings for anti-aircraft guns and radar. "Roofs" at ground level could be moved back hydraulically to reveal guns and target-acquisition radar. To a Soviet reconnaissance plane, they would have looked like a bunch of residential streets.

The author remembers walking down to this area with his grandfather in about 1953 and inquiring about what was here. We were told to leave by an armed sentry. There were anti-aircraft emplacements in Englewood Cliffs, Teaneck, Union City, Fort Schuyler, Queens, Fort Hamilton, Brooklyn, and Sandy Hook, NJ. A concealed anti-aircraft post remained here until about 1955. The gun batteries were replaced by anti-aircraft missiles relocated to the vicinity of Mahwah, Morristown, and Wayne, because the missiles had greater range.

In the 19th century, there were few side streets. Balsam, Spruce, and Aspen were off Englewood Avenue; Pomander Walk was Riverside Avenue and Kipp Avenue, depending on which part you were in. Fycke Lane was originally called Parker Lane. There's another Parker Lane with the same owner/landlord on the other side of Teaneck Road. It became Fycke Lane sometime in the 19th century. The 1876 map shows that it ended down by Teaneck Creek, and the 1912 map has it just going through to Marion Street. The surrounding land had originally been owned by Benjamin Parker and had been sold off.

John Street was named after one of the first property owners to buy from Benjamin Parker.

John H.P. Zohnker was one of the first local greenhouse men in the 19th century. Around the turn of the 20th century, commercial greenhouses became a major Teaneck industry. Captain John Jay Phelps, son of William Walter Phelps, had commercial greenhouses at his estate, Red Towers, on River Road, where the Fairleigh Dickinson University campus now stands. Zohnker, who originally owned five acres, ended up with a lot more down through Glenwood Park. He grew ornamental flowers for weddings, meeting halls, hotels, and banquets in New York. He made a good living from it because of the proximity to Manhattan. German immigrants seemed to have a monopoly

Frank Letter's farmhouse, Fycke Lane

in the flower market.

Teaneck streets tend to be named after the first name (rather than the surname). Frank Letter's farmhouse at 175 Fycke Lane has a stone foundation. He bought the strip that goes from Thomas Jefferson School to the Overpeck. Dutch farms tended to be long and narrow. This was the site of worst fire in the area in terms of the number of buildings involved—about six. The fire, which started behind the Blue Bird Inn (the current Volks Funeral Home) on March 10, 1927, can be called a wildland–urban interface fire, like those in California. The clean-up man from the Inn had gathered the vegetable crates and burned them in the backyard, which was legal then. The fire started burning in a southeasterly direction. The Glenwood Park Hose Company #4, which only had a hose wagon, came up by Marion Street, stretched almost all their hose, and operated only with hydrant pressure. The water stream was not effective because of the high wind. The only pumper in Teaneck was Engine #1, which had to be driven across open fields from East Cedar Lane (where senior citizen housing is now) to boost the force of water. It was a long operation. Engine #1 got into an accident going through the muddy fields. When it finally reached the scene and hooked up into Company #4's line, the two stopped the fire, but by then six buildings had been destroyed.

As a result of this fire, the Teaneck mayor and council asked the fire department what they could do to prevent such disasters in the future. The basic problem was wood-shingled roofs, which are prone to catching embers and burning the building down. Teaneck and other towns added a ban on such shingles to their building codes in 1929, but the ban was partly undermined when the state government preempted local building codes in 1977.

Glenwood Park

The Glenwood Park neighborhood used to be like an island surrounded by swamps until better drainage was installed. The only way in or out by vehicle or foot was Marion Street; however, there was also the trolley. Hemlock Terrace, north and south, used to be called Railroad Avenue; the street cars that went from the 125th Street ferry in Edgewater to Paterson ran along it. The original name was the Hudson River Railroad, but it had several names throughout its history and wound up being owned by the Public Service Electric Company from 1906 on. It ran behind the Glenpointe parking garage, which had been meadows, made a turn on a private right-of-way, then crossed Teaneck Road and DeGraw Avenue. De Graw Avenue had been built extra wide to accommodate the double-track trolley lines on the inside and two lanes for cars on the outside. It crossed the Overpeck Creek at the golf course, where there was a turnbridge, then went onto a complex, spindly railroad trestle that carried it over the Erie Railroad and then up to Grand, to Hillside Avenue, and up Broad on its way to Fort Lee Road.

The trolley was started in the 1890s and came through this area in 1898.

Trolley Trestle from Leonia to Teaneck

Marine Court was a trolley company sandpit—the sand was needed to provide traction for the steel wheels against steel rails in rain and snow. All railroads had sand pits. It was a temporary construction yard for the trolley line, which was not built all in one piece. As fares and revenue increased, they could build the next bridge and terminal. In 1899, the trolley line ended at Palisade Avenue and Main Street in Bogota. Large reels of expensive copper cable were used to provide the overhead power contact for the cars stored in the construction yard. One night, someone stole a big reel, which even then was probably worth thousands of dollars. The thief was caught by a conductor and motorman who happened to be passing through on the way to Edgewater. The thief went to jail. His friends were enraged at this and decided to exact revenge. They obtained a copy of the staff roster and found out when the conductor and motorman would be working next. Unfortunately, they got it wrong. The fellows that they lay in ambush for would be coming through around midnight. They cut down trees and made a barricade across the tracks. The trolley had one passenger and the two-man crew. When they got to the obstruction, the crew got out to clear the way, and snipers opened up on them. The snipers were idiots because the first thing they shot was the trolley car headlight. The two crewmen backed the car up about three hundred feet and then crashed through the barricade, knocking it out of the way. The passenger was wounded by broken glass from a window. From a track-side telephone, the crew then called the dispatcher, who sent out all the workers out of the terminal—mechanics, car cleaners, and such—armed them with Winchester rifles. When they reached the trolley operators, they settled the matter without resort to police or courts.

The trolley figured in another episode on Hemlock Terrace. In

1928, the Ku Klux Klan was very powerful in the Glenwood Park section, where it predominantly opposed Catholics. Tremendous ethnic and religious tensions had traveled there from the Sudetenland, now part of the Czech Republic. People would wear unconcealed pistols on their belts, and it was not uncommon for them to draw their weapons and shoot at each other.

The Klan saw an opportunity to take advantage of the local tension in the 1928 election, in which, for the first time, a Roman Catholic, Al Smith of New York, was running for president. The idea of having an Irish Catholic president was unacceptable to many, and the ranks of the Klan swelled. A local chapter was started, which first exacerbated the local ethnic and religious trouble and then tried to interfere in the Democratic primary.

At that point, a black Baptist minister from Shore Avenue in Leonia, unconnected with the local problems, found a house for sale on Hemlock Terrace that he wanted to turn into an outreach chapel. The Klan initially decided to dynamite the building. They had done so to other buildings, but this one was too close to the houses of sympathizers. Instead, they decided to use the trolley to demolish the structure. A cow was put across the track at the edge of the woods, so that the westbound trolley would have to stop. When the crew got out to move the cow, two men remonstrated with them while another Klansman put a wrecking chain around what he thought was the main support of the house and hooked it to the back bumper of the trolley. After a signal, his buddies moved the cow. The crew got back in and had to build up considerable speed because it was a steep incline, but the Klansman had not attached the chain correctly and succeeded only in pulling the porch off the house.

Another time, a local man who was having financial problems

decided to dynamite his house an make it look as if the Klan was responsible. He planned to go to a local speakeasy on Fycke Lane, get lubricated with drink, bad-mouth the Klan, then call his home and set off the TNT. But while he was doing the wiring in his basement for the explosion, a telemarketer called and blew him out of the basement. He later confessed.

Glenwood and Hemlock Terrace North had several Glenwood Park general stores, an unofficial trolley station, candy stores, and a luncheonette. At Glenwood and Terrace South, now occupied by a white house, stood a fire station (#4) from 1913 to 1940, and an ambulance station (1940–1948). In 1948, it became a furniture warehouse, which burned down in 1961, scorching several surrounding buildings and igniting a huge brush fire in the meadows by ember extension.

In 1911, the fire company had only a hand-drawn hose wagon, and one of three ladder trucks. The other two were at Teaneck and Fairview and at New Bridge Road. More fire companies were necessary then because the apparatus was drawn by firefighters who, exhausted after about ten blocks, then had to extinguish the blaze. The Teaneck Volunteer Ambulance Corps was born here, where the ambulance was housed here at night from 1940 to 1948; during the day, it was parked by the police station.

On the site of Glenwood and Fabry Terrace stood Joseph Kennedy's blacksmith shop, which was important to community life. The first meeting to establish a fire company in 1911 was held there, as were other group meetings, such as those of a boy's club. It was the social heart of Glenwood Park. The building burned down in 1941. Behind the trolley site was a church, essentially comprising a complete community. Most Teaneck neighborhoods were like that at the close of the 19th century.

The original Public Service trolley right-of-way, from 1899 to 1938, came through the meadows. A wooden bridge used to cross Teaneck Creek behind the Glenpointe parking garage. This was very steep for a trolley. From there, it went up DeGraw Avenue, which used

Trolley Station, DeGraw and Teaneck Road

to stop one block east of Teaneck Road, where there had been a large greenhouse. The land for the line had been bought by private landowners and had a regular railroad right-of-way, just as a first-class railroad would have had. Where the private right-of-way ended at DeGraw, the trolley went onto public streets and ran through Teaneck, Bogota, and Hackensack. In Teaneck and Bogota, the land was donated to the township by William DeGraw, a wealthy farmer descended from a line of prosperous farmers originally who originally lived in Fort Lee and then relocated to Teaneck. The current fire Station #3 is on the site of DeGraw's farm house. On the day that the trolley service was inaugurated, he slipped off the step of the trolley, cut his leg, and subsequently died of septicemia.

The private right-of-way was called Flicks Road, after the John R. Flick construction company, which used part of the right-of-way after 1938.

The house at 300 Teaneck Road is from the 1830s and belonged to a Mrs. Van Winkle. Teaneck Road had a series of these large houses, on huge lots, from Fort Lee Road to the Bergenfield border. Some are in the Dutch colonial style, e.g., the one at the foot of Copley and Van Buren. Above Cedar Lane, there was a continuous row of houses with about eighteen to twenty rooms each, a size that prevailed throughout the town. One of them belonged to Lebeus Chapman, who resembled Audubon in his depiction of birds and who was a founder of the American Museum of Natural History in New York. One of Teaneck's first public schools, at 381 Fort Lee Road, dates from the mid-19th century—probably about the 1830s. It served the south end of Teaneck, Ridgefield Township, Bogota, Leonia, and Ridgefield Park. There is another house, a small brown one, at 374 Fort Lee Road, which was part of the teacher's pay.

Nineteenth-century teacher's house, Fort Lee Road School

Before 1859, there was no public transportation of any kind in Bergen County except for the stagecoach from Hackensack to Hoboken, but that came nowhere near the school, so children had to walk or take farm wagons.

Fort Lee Road used to go through from Hackensack to Fort Lee. It was built by a private sector turnpike company in 1824 to make a direct connection from Fort Lee to Hackensack. In 1869, it became a public road, owned by the county, and it ran through until 1960. Now it is just the access to the newly developed section of the Overpeck Park. When Route 80-95 was being planned and it became necessary to relocate the public road, DeGraw became the through street, and Fort Lee Road was dead- ended. There were several corner gas stations, and the area became a blossoming neighborhood for the car industry. On a nice day, motorists would be stuck in traffic here. Traveling to New York before the George Washington bridge was built entailed coming down Fort Lee Road (there were no Routes 4, 46, or 80), and through Bogota, Teaneck, Leonia, and Fort Lee to the Edgewater ferry, to 125th Street in New York. Most communities had a strong system of special part-time police— "straw hat cops", so-called because they were needed only on nice days. Their function was to control traffic at clogged intersections.

Fort Lee Road became a major commercial street with the advent of the automobile, with an auto parts store and repair garages. Cars were usually stored indoors in 1920 because the materials from which they were built could easily be destroyed by rain if left outside. Fort Lee Road had several indoor parking garages, since most people did not buy houses with garages. There would be six or eight gas stations in the space of five blocks. Gasoline is now stored in fiberglass tanks but used to be contained in steel, buried in cinders that turned to acid because the cinders contained the sulfur that had been in coal.

The Enke's Florist family came here before World War I and built greenhouses that went down to Park Avenue. When the Great War ended, a lot of buildings could be purchased from Camp Merritt in Dumont and moved. Enke relocated several large mess halls, encased them in glass, and used them to produce flowers from commercial markets. Damrau, a competitor, was around the corner at 375 Queen Anne Road. Gulden, the mustard king, also had growing areas on Fort Lee Road.

In the 18th and 19th centuries, people operated stores in Teaneck out of the front parlors of their houses. The first purpose-built store, constructed in 1908, was a butcher's shop at 110 Fort Lee Road. Another, at 112 Fort Lee Road, served as a grocery.

Teaneck did not have a fire-alarm system until 1937. Box # 37 at Fort Lee Road and Queen Anne was installed in that year at 2 p.m. At 3 p.m., a signal was received from the box and saved the building, Reinhardt's Pharmacy, from a working fire.

Appendix I

A Brief History of the Teaneck Fire Department

THE FIRST KNOWN ORGANIZED FIRE PROTECTION in Teaneck was provided by the Hackensack Township Protection Society, a part-paid, part-volunteer police organization that also provided organization and equipment for citizens to use in their own rudimentary fire defense. Prior to 1888, the equipment consisted of leather buckets, ladders, lanterns, and axes, stored loose. In 1871, Hackensack organized an engine company with a hand-drawn, hand-operated pumper. They responded to what is now Teaneck, but with astronomical response times due to poor roads and steep hills. The Englewood Fire Department also responded to 19th-century fires in Teaneck, with similar response-time problems. Both fire departments responded to the acetylene explosion and fire that destroyed the massive Phelps mansion at Cedar Lane and Teaneck Road on April 1, 1888. They removed art treasures ahead of the main body of fire in the mansion and effectively protected the Phelps stables west of the main fire building. One Hackensack volunteer firefighter was injured in a fall from a ladder at the stables.

The first organized fire company in Teaneck was Defender Hook and Ladder Company, quartered at about 722 New Bridge Road and providing first-due fire protection in New Bridge, lower New Milford, and the Cherry Hill section of River Edge. This company was formed on August 12, 1895, in response to the lack of organized rescue service during the Cherry Hill tornado. The company did not join the other four Teaneck fire companies when the municipal fire department was organized in 1915. Instead, it helped supply the nucleus for New Milford Fire Company 2, although it continued to respond in Teaneck until 1933.

In 1904, residents of the Manhattan Heights and Selvage developments formed the Upper Teaneck Volunteer Fireman's Association, taking possession of a five-hundred-foot hose reel, a nine-hundred-foot hose reel, four nozzles, some lanterns, and a life net owed to Teaneck from Englewood Township due to the municipal break-up of 1895. They also purchased a village-style ladder truck from Ladder Company 1 in Ridgefield Park. They were quartered in a two-storey flat-roofed white concrete-block fire station at 1188 Teaneck Road. The hose reels were both hand drawn and operated from the recently installed fire hydrants through two-and-a-half hose through smoothbore nozzles. The men were all volunteer, but the horses for the ladder truck were paid-on-call. When the gongs hit, the milk team, ice team, and mail team would all head for the fire station. The first team to connect to the ladder truck would get the run, and fifty cents. In 1907, this company ran into a major disagreement with their landlord, Walter Selvage. He claimed that the firefighters only had the right to be in quarters for alarms and scheduled meetings. The firefighters expressed their need for training and administrative time. As a result, they abandoned the beautiful fire station, which became Kobbe and Flannery's garage. Instead, they purchased a barn on Lafayette Place in Englewood, cut it in half, hired twenty mules, and cut a corduroy road through the future Argonne Park to drag it to 14 through 18 Fairview Avenue. They also obtained a touring car, donated by the widow

Phelps, did their own body work, and built a German-style Dividor hose reel car capable of laying hose on the fly, or of easily dismounting the reel and rapidly laying hose by hand across fields, lawns, etc. This was Teaneck's first motor fire apparatus. The station remained fire headquarters until 1920. It is now a multiple dwelling.

Meanwhile, in 1907, residents of the Bogota Park section inaugurated the Cedar Hill Volunteer Firemen's Association, also equipped with a hand-drawn hose reel. From 1907 to 1913, they responded from a member's barn on Linden Avenue. They then relocated to a new fire station at 513 Kenwood Place and remained there until 1953. This building is now the Chabad House. In 1908, Teaneck firefighters from Fairview Avenue helped save Englewood from a conflagration when gale-driven fire devoured a lumberyard, a livery stable, and the Hygiea Ice Works on South Van Brunt Street. When the ice works burned, a tank of anhydrous ammonia was released. This was the first known hazardous materials incident for the Teaneck Fire Department. The fire was stopped when Teaneck got a powerful hand-line to work.

In 1911, the residents of southern Teaneck formed the Teaneck Hose Company 1, responding with a hand-drawn hose reel from a member's barn on Teaneck Road until 1913, when the unique fire station at 395 Morningside Terrace was built in kit form by the members. The station was unique because, for runs west of the station, the hose reel on the main floor was dragged out onto Morningside Terrace, then called Elm Terrace. For runs east of the station, another hose reel came out of the basement and down a driveway to Fenimore Road. Also, this outstation had its own outstation. This station was used until November 1990 and is now being converted to a two-family dwelling. A garage at the Damrau greenhouses at 375 Queen Anne Road was rented to store yet another hose reel and a very heavy three-section, forty-five-foot wooden extension ladder designed to serve the burgeoning south Queen Anne Road business district

Also in 1911, the Glenwood Park Volunteer Fireman's Association was started, using a well-designed, four-wheel, hand-drawn "spider wagon." For two years, they were quartered in Kennedy's blacksmith shop at Glenwood and Fabry. Then they relocated to their new quarters at Glenwood and Railroad (now Hemlock Terrace South). This station remained in service until 1948, when it was converted into the Ronald's Furniture Warehouse; it burned down in a spectacular fire in November 1961.

In 1915, four of Teaneck's five independent volunteer fire companies were combined into the official municipal Teaneck Fire Department. Kenloch V. Ridley, of East Forest Avenue, an engineer with the New York Telephone Company, became Chief of Department. All members remained volunteer, but the township started paying for various expenses, including rent on the four fire stations. The Fairview Avenue fire station became Fire Company 1, and Kenwood Place became Fire Company 2. Morningside Terrace became Fire Company 3, and Glenwood Park became Company 4. Defender Hook and Ladder, in New Bridge, remained independent until disbanding.

During the period from the turn of the century to World War I, the Ayers and Lozier partnership developed the residential area north of West Englewood Avenue between Windsor and Essex. A private fire station, with a hand-drawn hose reel, existed at Rugby and Rutland to provide protection during construction. Construction workers were supposed to man this rig, but local tradition has it that they rarely turned out. Instead, volunteer firefighters from the other four companies, working their jobs as ice men, mailmen, and DPW workers in the area, usually took the reel to fires.

During this period, a very tough basement fire occurred on Maitland Avenue. Future Deputy Chief Harry Davis, then a DPW worker, made numerous entries, without breathing apparatus, manning a two-and-a-half-inch line, passing out repeatedly, being revived by the back-pressure arm-lift method, then going back in until the house was saved. Teaneck has always been an aggressive-attack, inside fire department.

In 1920, major improvements were made to the Teaneck Fire Department. A new fire headquarters was built at 1217 Teaneck Road, now the Sunrise Vulcanizing Company. Reo Speed Wagon hose trucks with chemically powered water tank systems were issued to companies 2, 3, and 4. A gasoline-driven triple-combination pumper built by American La France was assigned to the new fire headquarters. The Chief, K.V. Ridley, was granted an annual salary equal to half that of a police patrolman. A paid driver was hired to work an eight-hour day for the new pumper. The plan was to add one paid firefighter a year, all to headquarters.

The fire alarm system also had a major upgrade. Until 1920, a citizen or police patrol discovering a fire went to one of about forty fire gongs located at prominent street corner locations. A bent, discarded locomotive steel tire hanging from a wooden frame would be struck by a hammer according to instructions on an enameled sign posted at each location. For instance, the user of the fire alarm at Glenwood and Railroad would be told to hit the gong five times, then three times, then once, and repeat this complete signal, Box 531, four times. Other people throughout Teaneck who heard this signal were obligated to hit the nearest fire gong in the same way, alerting all volunteer members and the paid-on-call horse teams.

In 1920, two fire phones were installed to receive phone calls from the public in fire headquarters. Leased lines were connected to sound

World War I surplus air raid sirens at the four firehouses. Residents, then as now, were instructed to call the Fire Department, *not* the police, to report fires. Dedicated phone lines were established to the four firehouses and, eventually, to police headquarters. Red oak tag four-by-five-inch signs were printed up telling residents how to report a fire. Three of the volunteer companies willingly distributed these door to door; unfortunately, Company 3 refused to do so. A fire broke out in a house during a weekday at Hickory and DeGraw. Callers in that neighborhood did not know how to report the fire, so calls were relayed in error to Bogota Police and Hackensack Fire Departments before being correctly routed to Teaneck Fire Headquarters. A very obese woman was trapped at a second-floor front window. Floyd Farrant, a local businessman and volunteer firefighter, happened by and ascended the porch roof. He struggled by himself to pull the huge woman through the window, but the room flashed over, killing the screaming woman and burning Farrant's eyes, permanently blinding him. The nearest unit, Company 3, never responded. When headquarters, and the 2s and 4s, arrived, it was too late. Support for the volunteer fire department went into a nose dive.

The 1920s saw several other disastrous fires in town. In 1922, ashtrays carelessly dumped into a garbage can after a PTA meeting caused a late night fire in Longfellow School. Chief Ridley was on sick leave. The assistant chief took over but was later accused of a serious lack of leadership that was partly to blame for near-fatal injuries to a volunteer firefighter who went down with a floor collapse while doggedly pressing an interior attack. Other problems resulted when a ladder was ordered moved, cutting off a party of Hackensack firefighters attempting to open the roof. Since pumping power available to Teaneck and surrounding towns was slight compared to the size of the fire, a mutual aid call was placed to New York City. FDNY Engine Companies 58 and 36 responded via the 130th Street–Edgewater Ferry. Since New York does not use national standard fire hose thread, they could not use a hydrant. Instead, they drafted from a flooded gas company excavation at Teaneck and Oakdene. The school was destroyed.

Three women using gasoline to clean rugs in a corn crib were killed by fire at Teaneck and Blauvelt. Illegal alcohol distilleries exploded and burned on Carlton Terrace, Sheppard Avenue, Palisade Avenue, and New Bridge Road. A fire in staff quarters at the Nelden Sanitarium, a private hospital on Englewood Avenue and Nelden Road, killed the elderly mother of the proprietor and horribly burned her sister and a young doctor who had bravely entered to rescue them. On March 10, 1927, a "wildland-urban interface" conflagration started from a legal rubbish fire behind the Blue Bird Inn restaurant (and speak-easy) at 789 Teaneck Road. Dry northwest winds drove the fire eastward across open fields, jumping Lindberg Boulevard. Hose Company 4 made a valiant attempt to stop the raging brush fire at Fycke and Grant, but the nine-hundred-foot hose stretch uphill at only hydrant pressure, with the nozzle facing into a gale wind, resulted in an ineffective stream. Teaneck's only pumper tried to drive through deep mud from the Lewis farm on East Cedar Lane across open fields to reach Hose 4's hydrant to boost pressure on their defensive line. The slippery, ubiquitous mud caused an accident, and by the time the pumper reached the hydrant, three houses and three barns had been incinerated.

Clearly, stronger fire defenses were needed. Teaneck was growing, with a major lumberyard installed on Water Street in 1927, as well as four- and five-storey apartment houses going up in northeast and southwest Teaneck.

Different answers came from different sectors. In 1929, the Teaneck Chamber of Commerce and the *Teaneck Times* newspaper launched an eventually successful campaign for a municipal fire alarm system, with fire alarm boxes available to the public, and township-owned wires and cables to bring dispatch messages to the fire stations. A coded whistle signal, sounding the box number nearest the fire, replaced the unspecific sirens. These major improvements came to fruition between 1932 and 1937. The first box alarm came from Box 35, then at Fort Lee and Queen Anne, for a working fire in the Rexall Drugstore. This was pulled one hour after the box was placed in service. The store was saved. This excellent system survives in advanced form today and will, hopefully, far into the future.

In 1926, a "city-service" ladder truck, with hand-raised ladders but no aerial ladder, replaced the horse-drawn truck. In 1929, instead of adding just one paid man, six were hired, and a newer, more powerful pumper was purchased. To some, this was not enough. Councilman Fred Andreas declared, "The day of the volunteer fire department is done". In 1930, the Council hired Francis X. Murray as Deputy Fire Commissioner, with the responsibility of providing fire training and setting up a stronger fire-prevention program. Chief Ridley was vulnerable in both areas. While he was credited with excellent leadership at fires, he was accused of delegating training solely to the officers of the individual companies, never holding multi-unit drills. Likewise, Teaneck had had a fire prevention code since 1920, but the Chief was the only designated enforcer, with enforcement upon complaint only, with *no* proactive inspections. Some volunteer firemen, using their own time and money, had attended the New Haven Fire Department drill school, and had used their advanced knowledge to save the multiple dwelling at 17 West Englewood Avenue the night the Conrad Jordan mansion at 1380 Teaneck Road burned. Murray, a former traveling salesman for the American LaFrance Fire Engine Company, brought his traveling fire school to permanent roost, along with similar big-city fire training, with the local volunteer and paid firefighters. Now nightly classroom and drill school work was applied to the whole department. More paid men were added, until the department reached its present form in 1940.

In 1933 and 1934, a series of disastrous fires struck expensive, newly built Tudor style dwellings west of Garrison Avenue between Cumberland Avenue and Route 4. The Meszick homes burned night after frigid night from failure to provide eight inches of solid masonry between the brand-new fireplaces and the wooden wall studs above the mantels. Women and children leaped from upper floor windows, pursued by flames. A recently renovated six-unit multiple dwelling burned at 262 DeGraw Avenue due to insufficient clearance between the boiler breeching and wooden floor joists.

The public was rightfully outraged. The Building Department was accepting permit fees but was obviously not providing competent inspections. Realizing that firefighters whose lives are on the line were unlikely to be so lax, in 1933, the mayor and council ordered Deputy Fire Commissioner Murray and the Teaneck Fire Department to be proactive in plans for review and inspection of new construction—an aggressive life-saving program that thrives to this day despite continued opposition from special interests. Maintenance inspections of existing buildings also became a part of Teaneck Fire Department routine, with on-duty members detailed to walk the business districts with violations books, from the 1930s onward. With strict fire prevention, the endless parade of fire deaths and destroyed homes and businesses diminished.

During the 1930s, on-duty paid members constructed thirty-five miles of fire alarm wires, connected forty boxes, built a modern rescue truck out of an abandoned bus chassis, refurbished an eighty-five-foot aerial truck purchased from New York City, upgraded two existing pumpers, built one of New Jersey's few searchlight trucks, and renovated fire Stations 2 and 3 to accommodate paid personnel. In 1937, a pioneer two-way radio system was installed, far ahead of most cities. Stolen Nazi secrets led to Teaneck Fire Department firefighters being equipped with dry chemical fire extinguishers years before these devices were common.

When World War II loomed, the Teaneck Fire Department was in high gear. The remaining volunteer firemen either were inducted as paid firefighters, formed the Teaneck Volunteer Ambulance Corps, or joined the new Teaneck Fire Auxiliaries, who eventually became the present Box 54 organization. Trailer pumps were obtained, and a fire station was temporarily established at the Whittier School. Air raid drills were held among the various public safety organizations. Communications checks occurred every two hours. All this preparedness paid off on May 24, 1942, when two U.S. Army Air Force P-39 Aero-cobras collided in high winds over Teaneck Road and State Street. One plane dove out of control into the street in front of 1090 Dartmouth Street, spraying the front of a doctor's home with flaming aviation gas. Fire entered an open bedroom window where a little girl was sleeping. The other war plane spun towards Cherry Lane and Queen Anne Road, its gun solenoids shorted, spewing .50-caliber machine gun rounds from its guns. It hit the detached two-car garage at 890 Queen Anne Road, igniting the structure and two cars. The well-oiled public safety machine swung into action, instantly squelching both fires, rendering aid to two injured firefighters, an air raid warden, and the two pilots, and controlling crowds and traffic. The Teaneck Fire Department was so well prepared that Murray, now Chief of Department, offered to form a fire column to be loaded on landing ships and sent to Britain to fight the conflagrations spawned by the Luftwaffe!

Teaneck's tremendous growth after World War II, combined with exceptional prosperity, led to the construction of the present Fire Headquarters in 1948, followed by the present Fire Station 2 in 1953. The fire alarm system was improved, and many boxes were added. The idea of connecting building fire protection systems to Fire Headquarters via master fire alarm boxes was instituted locally in 1948, with the various schools being the first connected. Modern pumpers, the first since 1929, were added in 1947 and 1948, with a modern steel aerial ladder in 1949. Upgrades in the 1950s included a fifty-six-hour work week for firefighters, a switch to FM two-way radios, self-contained breathing apparatus to replace 1920s filter masks, and a more advanced rescue truck. The Glenwood Avenue fire station was closed, but a second ladder company was staffed at the new Cedar Lane fire station. In 1968, a permanent fire station in northwest Teaneck, desired since 1929, was opened, becoming Engine Company 4. New pumpers in 1959 and 1964, and two in 1968, as well as a 1965 aerial ladder, replaced older vehicles. In 1970, the work week was finally reduced to the present forty-two hours. The 1970s commenced with a near conflagration at the Teaneck Lumber Company on Water Street. Desperate work in an ice storm saved the surrounding business blocks on Cedar Lane and Front Street (now American Legion Drive). A mansion fire at 283 Barr Avenue in 1972 saw firefighters jumping from windows to avoid flaming floor collapses, but the building was saved, just as it had been from a similar fire in 1933. Three firefighters were burned when a fire in concealed spaces blew down explosively on them at the Figuretone Salon fire at Cedar and Garrison. Two of them narrowly escaped death. Major store fires in Sharban Carpets and the Davis Pool store threatened the Teaneck Theater, hurt dozens of firefighters, and wrecked neighboring Tabatchnik's delicatessen during this period. The Ronald's Furniture store burned down across from the municipal building.

The Teaneck Redevelopment Agency started accumulating houses in Glenwood Park to make way for Glenpointe. In 1976, Teaneck had a hundred and fifty structure fires, including thirty-six working fires in the blocks bounded by Glenwood, East Oakdene, and Harding Avenues and Division Street. Vandalism arson was rampant. Surely something had to be done.

In 1977, a new fire inspector was appointed, and two new programs grew rapidly. In 1974, Firemen's Mutual Benevolent Association Local 42 had started an aggressive public fire- safety information program. In 1977, this was made a department program, with fifty speeches and numerous news releases designed to inform the public how specifically to prevent accidental fires. For intentional fires, both structure and brush, a new Fire Department investigation program was launched. Every fire resulting in casualties or significant loss was instantly investigated by Fire Department personnel, sometimes while the fire was still raging. Local police at that time seemed reluctant to help, so the Teaneck Fire Department reached out directly to the Prosecutor's Office; the U.S. Bureau of Alcohol, Tobacco and Firearms; the New Jersey Forest Fire Service; and insurance investigators. Teaneck Fire Department stakeouts were set, informants cultivated, and patterns analyzed. Soon, arson profiteers were not getting their "sure thing" insurance payments, and juvenile delinquents were caught in their acts of vandalism. While punishments were still ridiculously small compared to the enormity of a fire, the certainty of capture had its effect, and the arson epidemic, both in buildings and in meadowlands, dramatically receded. Brush fires now are a mere ten percent of what they were. Building fires have declined by about a third, with arson much less of a problem. New apparatus, including four pumpers, a medium-duty rescue truck, and a tower ladder, were purchased in the 1980s. In 1990, a new Fire Station 3, at 370 Teaneck Road, replaced the decrepit Morningside Terrace fire station.

The lessons of ninety-nine years of organized fire protection are clear. The four fire stations are staffed twenty-four hours a day, and an adequate level of staffing, strict proactive code enforcement, the advanced municipal fire alarm system, and the aggressive fire-investigation programs are all absolutely necessary answers to very real, life-threatening problems. They must be maintained and improved far into the 21st century, so that Teaneck does not sink into the immense fire tragedies of the 1920s or the vast commercial fire losses of the 1970s.

Appendix II

Personal Railroad Memories Teaneck, 1950–1960

LOCOMOTIVES WERE WOOD-BURNING steam engines from 1873 to 1888. The first two "Grayson Place" bridges were burned down due to firebrands exhausting from locomotive stacks. From then until the 1950s, steam locomotives burned safer coal. My first household task as a child was to attend to the window sills after a steam locomotive passed, using a damp rag to mop up the soot left behind. By the 1950s, we all got used to the smell of (cleaner) diesel oil.

The Teaneck Station was located at the foot of Frances Street. There was a private sidewalk that ran from the station to Palisade Avenue near Merrison Street. The Township *voluntarily* plowed the sidewalks along Palisade Avenue from Cedar Lane to north of Cherry Lane. In the 1950s, our family had a brave, generous red-and-white tom cat named Skeeter. Around 7:15 p.m. the cat would go down to the station walkway and wait in the bushes for my dad to get off the train. He would then proudly and affectionately greet him and curl around his feet, purring, all the way home. When rail service was discontinued, he transferred his cat services to the bus stop.

Freight car arrivals at the team track at the foot of Merrison Street were job opportunities for the older boys and teenagers. Business owners were pressed to unload arriving cars quickly or face dunnage (storage) fees. Anyone willing to work could get at least fifty cents an hour. I remember stripping cars of Christmas trees, sheetrock, milled lumber, and school supplies for various local businesses.

Railroad safety practices were different before modern technology took hold. There was a crew of three in the locomotive—an engineer, a fireman, and a brakeman. The caboose, a crew car at the end on a freight train, contained the conductor (train commander), a brakeman, and a flagman. Despite the terminology, a few of these workers were women. The flagman's job was to drop off several hundred feet when a train was halting and use flags, flares, and red lanterns to prevent a rear-end accident with a following train. One device they used was a "railroad torpedo", a firework that was strapped to the rail behind a stopped train. If nothing else worked, the crew of a following train would hear a load explosion and apply the brakes just in time. As a kid I happily heard the torpedoes explode numerous times, but there were no rear-end railroad wrecks.

There were a few railroad accidents in Teaneck. One was a serious accident on the curve just above Tryon Avenue West in the 1930s. Although all the old-timers remembered it, there is no record in either the Teaneck Fire Department or Teaneck Volunteer Ambulance Corps records. In 1938, a beloved, hearing-impaired vegetable merchant, with an elderly horse drawing his wagon, was crossing the last grade crossing at West Englewood Avenue. Both the human and the horse failed to respond to the crossing bells and the whistle of the approaching train. Both were killed in a horrible collision witnessed by numerous school kids on their way home. The emotional reaction to this accident spelled the end of the grade crossing and spawned the existing pedestrian underpass. Also in the '50s, early on a summer evening, my grandfather came home and asked me to follow him. He had heard about a railroad accident. He took me to the foot of Terhune Street, where an empty boxcar was lying on its right side in the ditch where the lumber yard lead met the main southbound local track. Vandals had released the hand brake and gotten the car moving down the grade. Just before the main track, a railroad safety device called a "derailer" was in place, protecting the through-track from just such runaway cars. It had done its job and pitched the dangerous loose car aside, out of the way of fast through-trains.

A more serious piece of sabotage happened in September 1960. There was a perverse Teaneck tradition of juveniles working a major piece of destruction, on the night before school that had started as a means of protest against going back to school. Although this tradition had mainly manifested itself in large grass fires and fires in vacant buildings, by 1960 it had become more vicious and had included arson to an occupied house on Oakdene Avenue filled with sleeping children. This trend culminated at a track switch on the eastern track at the foot of Van Delinda Avenue. The switch serves the factory at 520 Palisade Avenue. Persons unknown broke the brass switch lock and partly unset the switch from main line to industrial track. They then tied a rope to the switch handle and waited for a southbound train. They let the engine and the first ten and a half cars pass the switch, and then they threw it, so that the front wheels of the eleventh car followed the main line, and the rear wheels started up the hall to the factory, turning that car into a "snow plow" that mowed down railroad communications poles and small trees. The next ten freight cars violently derailed and spewed out their contents. Fortunately, there were no hazardous materials. The right-of-way was strewn with whole frozen beef carcasses, lumber, and coal. The only call to the municipal services came from a resident on Terhune Street reporting a "car blocking the railroad tracks". The caller said nothing about a wrecked railroad car. Police, reasonably assuming that a parked automobile had slipped its brakes, sent only a special park policeman to set out flares. He was astonished to find a major train wreck. Teaneck turned the incident over to the railroad, as there had been no injuries, no hazards, and the only damage had been on and to railroad property. When railroad authorities arrived the next morning, perhaps not so astonishingly, almost all the spilled cargo had been cleaned up by looters.

www.ingramcontent.com/pod-product-compliance
Lightning Source LLC
Chambersburg PA
CBHW051804040426
42446CB00007B/516